NORTH UIST
Lochmaddy
Little Minch
Uig
Balivanich
Dunvegan
Portree
SOUTH UIST
Skye
Lochboisdale
Broadford
Kyle of Lochlash
BARRA
Castlebay
Armadale
RUM
Mallaig
EIGG
Arisaig
Barra Head
Ardnamurchan Point
Arinagour
COLL
Tobermory
Scarinish
TIREE
Salen
Craignure
Mull
IONA
Firth of Lorn
COLONSAY
Jura
Islay
Port Askaig
Craighouse
Bowmore
Port Ellen
Campbeltown
Ireland
Aultbea
Gairloch
Kinlochewe
Shieldaig
Applecross
Lochcarron
Achnasheen
Garve
Dingwall
Muir of Ord
Beauly
Inverness
Dornoch
Tain
Alness
Invergordon
Cromarty
Moray Firth
Ardersier
Nairn
Elgin
Peterhead
Grantown on Spey
Carrbridge
Aviemore
Glen
Fort Augustus
Kingussie
Newtonmore
Ben Macdui
Aberdeen
Great
Corpach
Spean Bridge
Dalwhinnie
Fort William
Ben Nevis
Strontian
Kinlochleven
Ballachulish
Lochaline
Oban
Tyndrum
Dalmally
Inveraray
Arrochar
Lochgilphead
Dunoon
Gourock
Wemyss Bay
Tarbert
Rothesay
BUTE
Firth of Clyde
Millport
Ardrossan
Brodick
ARRAN
Ayr
Dundee
Perth
Stirling
Firth of Forth
Edinburgh
Glasgow
0 20 40 60 km
0 10 20 30 40 ml
N

Highlands and Islands Development Board

FIFTEENTH REPORT

1 January 1980 to 31 December 1980

Presented to Parliament in pursuance of
Section 3(3) of the Highlands and Islands
Development (Scotland) Act 1965
Inverness May 1981

ISBN 0 902347 67 5

To the Right Honourable GEORGE YOUNGER, MP
Her Majesty's Secretary of State for Scotland

Sir
I have the honour to present the fifteenth report of the Highlands and Islands Development Board for the period 1 January 1980 to 31 December 1980.

I am Sir,
Your obedient servant

(Sgd.) DAVID A DUNBAR-NASMITH, Chairman

Highlands and Islands Development Board
Bridge House, 27 Bank Street, Inverness IV1 1QR
May 1981

Contents

Rear Admiral David Dunbar-Nasmith, Chairman

Foreword

It falls to me this year to write the foreword to the board's fifteenth Annual Report — the year 1980 and the last year of Sir Kenneth Alexander's highly successful chairmanship of the board. In doing this I am helped by having served as Deputy Chairman throughout Sir Kenneth's five years and for three and a half years before that with Sir Andrew Gilchrist. I have also learned much from the views expressed by the members of our Consultative Council over the last eight and a half years under the wise guidance of Lord Cameron and Sir Robert Grieve, himself the first Chairman of the board. This has taught me many things, but particularly that development is a continuing business, and that to be successful plans need to be clearly understood and supported by the people who are most likely to be affected.

New ideas are constantly required. Many will not come to fruition, but some will succeed. Those with the best chance of success are likely to be based on natural resources, but the biggest single factor in determining success is the personality and capability of the individuals carrying out the development. Therefore, no ideas should be lightly discarded. Even projects which have failed at one time may succeed on a future occasion due to changed circumstances or with different individuals in control.

When Parliament set up the Highland Board they stipulated that more than 50% of board members, including the Chairman, should be full-time. Over the years this has helped to create a sense of envolvement between board members and staff and the people of the Highlands and Islands. Few, if any, organisations have responsibilities covering such a wide range as every type of economic and social development, and in such a scattered geographical area which includes, in addition to many small and remote mainland communities, over fifty separate islands where people live and work throughout the year.

Such success as the board have managed to achieve in the last 15 years has, in my view, been due in no small measure to the fact that we are able to directly support developments of all kinds in a particular geographical area — industrial (from major projects to handicrafts), tourism (covering many different types of enterprises and their marketing), farming and horticulture, fishing boats, fish processing plants, sea angling, fresh water fishing and fish farming. Indeed, the only major development which the board cannot stimulate directly with financial assistance is forestry planting. Here the board rely on the Forestry Commission to plant at their own hand or to stimulate private planting in our area. For this reason we are concerned lest any changes in the powers, policies or procedures of the Forestry Commission should result in a reduction in the rate of planting in the Highlands and Islands. An increased rate of planting is required not only to bring long term advantages to the people of our area, but to build up the United Kingdom's timber stocks. No less than 59% of the Forestry Commission's reserves of plantable land in the United Kingdom lie in the Highlands and Islands.

In many ways 1980 has been a difficult year in the Highlands and Islands because of the recession in the United Kingdom and the world generally. Unemployment levels have increased, but to a lesser extent than in the rest of Scotland and the United Kingdom. For the first time since the war unemployment levels in the Highlands and Islands as a whole are less than in the rest of Scotland. It is difficult to take much comfort from a situation which is worse than it it was in 1979, particularly when so much remains to be done. Nevertheless, it is important to assess accurately where we stand and I believe that the Highlands and Islands are now well placed to take advantage of an upturn in the economy. There will be disappointments and failures ahead. One or two unmistakable signs are evident now, but in the long term prospects are not discouraging.

In spite of the recession the flow of applications for new projects and the expansion of existing businesses continue at a very satisfactory level and we are gradually building up a nucleus of modern factory and workshop premises in many different places in the area. In a few years time the availability of these factories should begin to be comparable with what exists in other parts of the country, but we still have some way to go. This resource is a critical factor in attracting industrial projects of the right size to places where they will ultimately make a significant social impact. Let there be no doubt about it, significant attractions are required if we are to combat the fundamental and inescapable difficulties of higher transport costs and distance from consumer markets.

The shutting of the pulp mill at Fort William has been a major blow to Lochaber and the board have mounted intensive efforts to help bring alternative forms of employment to the area. Exceptional problems require new and unusual approaches and the board have embarked on several of these. In the field of promotion we have tried many things over the years. By engaging Job Creation Ltd, Coopers and Lybrand Associates, as well as Venture Founders Corporation, we hope to achieve new and improved results. Time alone will tell. Whatever happens we shall keep trying.

In Shetland the run down of the oil industry construction phase and the change in the pattern of offshore servicing is going to require close attention and support for the traditional industries, if they are to regain the place they held on the island before the coming of oil.

The end of the year saw the Highland Craftpoint building at Beauly completed, the staff engaged and ready for the start of full operations. They have a highly professional job to do, providing technical advice and practical assistance to all aspects of craftwork with the clear aim of helping firms achieve commercial viability. Skill in marketing and administration is just as important as product development, training methods, design skills and production efficiency. With their inhouse and external services Highland Craftpoint will be able not only to help existing craft businesses survive and become more profitable, but to seek out ideas and people to start new businesses in as wide a craft field as possible.

The strength of the pound, increased price of petrol and the recession generally made it a difficult year for tourism, in spite of our great natural resources. The tourist is watching his money more closely, is reluctant to pay the increased prices which inflation has made necessary, is not travelling so far and is looking for value for money. The message from tourist operators is that standards must be high and at a realistic price if we are to maintain our share of tourist business available. The weather has not helped either. One of the wettest summers on record, followed by a relatively snowless winter, seems set to bring home in a brutal fashion the importance to Spey Valley of a year round season. In spite of this there are many applications for tourism developments and improvements in the pipeline, emphasising the importance which operators place on updating and improving their facilities and providing things for people to do. The 'activity holiday' is the 'in thing' for 1981.

The fishing industry has been fraught with uncertainty throughout 1980 creating severe problems for fishermen with heavy financial commitments to meet before they fully own their boats. Fishing boats and the shore side of the industry are of relatively greater importance and significance to most island communities than to the majority of mainland communities. Agreement on an EEC fishing policy has therefore been awaited with anxious concern. A bad bargain for Scotland could be catastrophic for the islands. One only has to see the difference in prosperity between those small islands that have a safe fishing harbour and those that do not, and it is for this reason that the board wish to see island harbours improved. The work going on at Port Ellen on Islay, for example, is much welcomed. There is, too, a pressing need to develop alternative catching areas relatively free from restrictions on traditional sources of fish supplies. We remain confident that there is a great natural resource of fish waiting to be caught west of the Hebrides, an area still very much under-fished by the UK fleet.

The development of fish farming has continued steadily during the year, with many projects expanding according to plan and many more new ones starting. The employment created, particularly in places where it is very difficult to create jobs by other means, is significant to the communities concerned. Further, as some farms get established and expand relatively more local employment is created. We have several research projects underway, which we hope may lead to viable smaller enterprises which can be undertaken by crofters and local people without the need for massive capital investment. Fish farming is still a high risk business and, in salmon in particular, competition from Norway is almost certain to increase greatly in the next few years. Salmon farmers are therefore going to have to find ways of producing a very high quality product more economically. In the board's view, there is a great need for co-operation in and concentration on marketing if the high promise expected from the fish farming industry is to be achieved. We still have great hopes for shellfish farming, but accept that it is running probably some ten years behind salmon and trout.

Continuing low market prices, high interest rates and poor weather made 1980 a particularly difficult year for farmers. The recent establishment of an EEC policy for sheep meat gives ground for some optimism, but it must be remembered that indebtness in the industry has never been so high.

A particular landmark in 1980 was the Government's anouncement that the offshore gas gathering pipeline system is to be built and a pipeline laid from St Fergus to transport some of this gas to Nigg Bay on the Cromarty Firth. This is a project for which we have worked for a number of years and brings a step nearer a considerable range of development opportunities for the Cromarty Firth. All of these will not necessarily come about and there is much to be done before we have in existence a substantial industrial base on the inner Moray Firth. Such an industrial base would enable most places in the Highlands to have relatively easy access to the type of commercial and professional services which today cannot be found closer to the Highlands than the central belt of Scotand. This has been a key stone in the board's strategy for the Highlands since we took office in 1965. The need today is as great as it was then.

Transport of all kinds will forever be of major significance to an area like the Highlands and Islands, and particularly for those who live on islands. The effect of inflation over the last ten years has on the whole been relatively more severe on rural routes, and by UK standards almost all transport services in the Highlands and Islands are rural routes. Some transport routes, especially international ones, are becoming cheaper through intense price competition, but domestically public transport fares often rise faster than prices in general. There has always been a degree of cross subsidisation in transport undertakings, whereby the more highly used systems tend to pay part of the costs of the less well used systems. It will be a bad day for the Highlands and Islands, and areas of the country with a small population, if limitation of overall budgets causes national transport systems to depart from these well established principles.

Meanwhile we are pleased to see that the Government have recently provided increased finance to maintain the present sea ferry services. The board have long supported the need for a road equivalent tariff, but we are also conscious that costs of sea ferry systems must be contained through rationalisation of ferry services as a whole. We have put forward long term proposals to encourage examination of shorter routes, cheaper terminals, standard ferry designs and route tendering for operations. Our area is very dependent on an effective network of air, rail and road services, at a realistic price, and this depends on economic operation of airfields, continuing investment in track and rolling stock, and containment of fuel cost increases.

The biggest single worry on the horizon is the cost of transport and this is outside the board's power to influence. Having said that, it is only fair for me to finish by saying that the board are greatly encouraged that in a period of financial stringency and close examination of public expenditure, our grant-in-aid has been maintained in real terms. We welcome the Government's action in maintaining this level of support for our work.

David Dunbar-Nasmith

The esplanade at Millport, in the Cumbraes, which became part of the board's area early in 1980.

Stocking of the board's deer farm at Rahoy Estate, in Morvern, was completed during 1980.

One of the most important projects assisted by the board during the year was the modernisation and re-equipment of the Kilmallie sawmill at Fort William.

Caithness Leather Products manufacture a range of leather goods in a board factory at Wick.

A nest of four workshop units on the Longman Industrial Estate, Inverness, which should be occupied early in 1981.

The marina at Loch Melfort in Argyll, the type of facility which the board hope will result from the water sports development strategy approved during the year for the Argyll and Bute district.

The new shop opened on Papa Westray by the Papay Community Co-operative.

The attractive tearoom in the new 'An Clachan' crafts centre built by the board at Leverburgh in Harris.

The refurbished Victorian railway station at Strathpeffer provides an attractive location for crafts workshops, a tourist information office and an interpretive centre.

The Brodick tourist office, built by the board for the Isle of Arran Area Tourist Organisation, won a commendation in the 1980 regional awards of the Royal Institute of British Architects.

A healthy rainbow trout from the fish farming research station operated by Fish Farm Developments at Stronachullin, Argyll.

Advance workshop units built by the board at Sandbank, Dunoon.

A custom built factory under construction for a new electronics company being assisted by the board in Rothesay, Isle of Bute.

Creels and allied products are being manufactured at Golspie in a new project assisted by the board in 1980.

The board and the regional economy

1 In recent years this assessment of the health of the Highlands and Islands economy has dealt with long-term trends in development. This year, however, it has been difficult to ignore short-term developments in the national economy and their implications for the Highlands and Islands. Nationally, 1980 saw industrial output by manufacturing industry fall to its lowest level since 1968. Most economic forecasts for 1981 predict a continuation of this decline and a consequent increase in the level of unemployment.

Effects of recession

2 Unemployment in the Highlands and Islands decreased slightly in the first half of the year but later rose to end the year 1.4% above the level of December 1979. However, the area did not feel the effects of recession as severely as other parts of the United Kingdom. Average unemployment remained below that of Scotland during 1980 and steadily improved against the average for Britain.

COMPARATIVE UNEMPLOYMENT NOT SEASONALLY ADJUSTED

		Highlands & Islands			*Scotland*			*GB*		
		M(%)	*F(%)*	*T(%)*	*M(%)*	*F(%)*	*T(%)*	*M(%)*	*F(%)*	*T(%)*
July	1979	8.7	7.3	8.3	9.0	7.2	8.3	6.6	4.8	5.9
December	1979	9.3	9.3	9.3	8.9	6.5	7.6	6.4	4.1	5.5
July	1980	9.2	7.4	8.5	11.5	9.0	10.5	8.7	6.2	7.7
December	1980	11.3	9.7	10.7	13.5	9.0	11.6	10.9	6.5	9.1
December	1980	8,915	4,627	13,542						

*Notes: Details by employment exchange area are given in Appendix 4.
Arran and the Cumbraes are excluded from the figures above.*

3 The worst of the national recession may yet hit the Highlands and Islands in 1981, but there are good reasons for believing that on this occasion the Highlands and Islands will be insulated to some extent from some of the more serious effects. In its structure of employment the area is less dependent upon the manufacturing sectors where the bulk of the impact on output and employment has been felt. In particular, it has a low proportion of employment in the manufacturing sectors which are suffering most, like steel, heavy engineering, artificial fibres and chemicals. Many of these industries, which provide basic products in the manufacturing process, have suffered from the magnified

effects of lower output and the reduction of stocks by other industries and suppliers. Where strong inter-industry links exist in the Highlands and Islands, these have been particularly with the oil industry which has been stimulated by higher energy prices during the year and continues at a high level of activity.

4 National economic statistics indicate that against the background of industrial decline, consumer expenditure rose in real terms during 1980 and is projected to continue increasing at a slow rate in 1981. The maintenance of this expenditure has benefitted the higher than average proportion of employment in consumer services in the Highlands and Islands, including tourist services. The resilience of consumer expenditure has also maintained the level of demand for agricultural products, together with the stimulus provided by the levels of intervention prices and support from European Economic Community and national agricultural policies.

Forecast

5 Some deterioration in the economic prospects for the area in 1981 can therefore be expected, but one similar to other recessions in the post-war period. Undoubtedly the strength of sterling will present problems for a number of manufacturing firms dependent upon export markets, and for the tourist industry. The oil industry may also provide less of a stimulus if oil prices are not allowed to increase in real terms, but in the Moray Firth this would be more than offset by the decision to link the Cromarty Firth with the proposed gas gathering system in the North Sea.

Investment

6 The relatively buoyant state of the Highlands and Islands economy in 1980 was reflected in the demand for assistance from the board in almost all sectors of activity. The board's main forms of financial assistance are loans, normally at a preferential rate of interest and repayable over periods of five to ten years, grants and share participation in companies.

7 In 1980 our investment in new and existing businesses throughout the Highlands and Islands amounted to £12.3 million. The contribution from private sources resulted in a total joint investment of £38 million which is expected to create or retain over 1,600 jobs. The assistance approved covered 737 projects which was 109 less than in the previous year, a not unexpected result in a period of severe recession.

8 Assistance approved by the board in the ten years from 1 January 1971 amounted to £118 million at 1980 prices, in respect of 4,778 projects, in which nearly 20,000 jobs were provided or retained. Of this, £48.7 million was in the form of grant and £69.3 million by way of loan, again all at 1980 prices. The corresponding funds from the private sector amounted to over £214 million. A detailed analysis of board assistance approved since 1971 is given in Appendix 5.

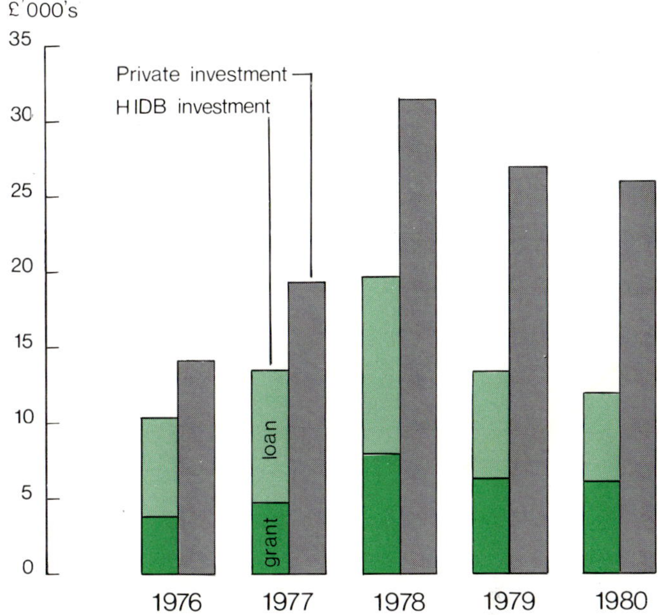

Loan repayment

9 From 1971 to 1980 loan repayments and interest received from businesses assisted totalled £16.3 million. All such receipts are re-invested in the area. Since 1 January 1971 the board have advanced loans totalling £29.3 million and during the same period some £1 million has been written off as irrecoverable. Provision for losses of loan capital of £770,000 was made in the board's accounts for the year ended 31 March 1980, representing 4.3% of the £18.1 million balance of loans outstanding at that date. At 31 December 1980 the balance outstanding stood at £20.3 million and in view of the continuing recession it is likely that an increase in the provision for loss will be required in the accounts for the financial year 1980/81.

10 A total of £318,000 has also been written off in respect of grants to businesses which had ceased to trade before expiry of the period of obligation to repay grants. Taking into consideration the adverse economic conditions prevailing in 1980 and the board's task of assisting in the development of one of the most difficult areas in Britain, we believe that the level of losses incurred are acceptable. Reasonable risks must be taken in backing promising business ventures which, without board assistance, might not become established. In every case projects are also backed by private capital.

After care

11 In addition to the investigation of applications for financial aid, staff are responsible for the monitoring of businesses already in receipt of assistance. Our 'after-care' involvement with such businesses begins as soon as the assistance is approved and we consider it vital that borrowers' problems

are identified and dealt with as quickly as possible. At the outset, applicants are advised to consult professional accountancy firms and make use of their services. We would again like to acknowledge the co-operation of the local professional firms and banks in augmenting our own services.

12 In addition to our normal monitoring activities we have a special management services unit. This unit, which is to be expanded, can provide a broader and more intensive range of management services to selected businesses.

Local impact

13 Historically the improvement in the relative position of the Highlands and Islands has been closely associated with the increase in the board's financial assistance and other development expenditure. It is, however, difficult to assess the changes which have taken place and prospects for the Highlands and Islands as a whole. In many respects it is a series of local economies linked not so much by their interdependence as an economic unit, but the extent to which they share common problems and dependence upon traditional sectors. In the board's first annual report this was reflected in the chairman's statement that 'No matter what success is achieved in the eastern or central Highlands... the board will be judged by its ability to hold population in the true crofting areas'.

14 Against that background, the board, therefore, monitor the trends and changes in the Highlands and Islands within 21 separate statistical areas. The shortage of official economic and social data makes it impossible for there to be a consistent set of statistics for these areas, but information is obtained from local sources and from the experience of board staff in working in these areas. In 1980 the board initiated reviews of each of the areas on a regular basis to summarise historical changes, the current position and the impact of board expenditure. The aim is to identify and follow up new development opportunities together with consideration of how the board can most effectively assist individual areas. This exercise will enable us, after the period of initial preparation, to review development progress in all parts of the Highlands and Islands on a regular and comparable basis.

15 This work is additional to and complements our continuing policy to improve information about and contact with all parts of the Highlands and Islands. In recent years this has included the reorganisation of financial investigation staff (as reported in 1977) on an area basis, and the increase in the number of staff outposted in local offices. This year the board also embarked on a second round of business seminars designed to encourage contact between board staff, the business community and representative bodies in local areas.

Special needs

16 There will always be a need for the board to give special attention to particular areas because of their special problems. One such area in 1980 was Lochaber, which suffered the shock of facing the closure of the pulp mill at Corpach. The closure came on top of the longer term problems, referred to in our 1978 report, of finding jobs for the children of families who moved into Lochaber in the 1960's. Full details of the board's special programmes in Lochaber are given in paragraphs 63 to 65.

17 Other areas facing equally severe problems of adjustment in the next few years are those with significant oil development. Some of them face a rundown in oil activity coupled with the reduction in assistance from losing their designation as Development Areas. Nairn district at the end of the year had an unemployment rate of 20% for males. Shetland's unemployment was still well below the Highlands and Islands average but the rundown of 4,000 jobs at Sullom Voe, and other developments such as the lessening dependence on Sumburgh air terminal, combine to create a need for careful anticipation of forthcoming adjustment problems.

Representations

18 The Highlands and Islands can be affected by a wide range of policies initiated by bodies at national or even international level, such as the European Economic Community. It is always necessary to keep these developments under review and, where appropriate, to make representations putting forward the special circumstances and case of the Highlands and Islands, which may otherwise be overlooked.

19 The board continue to keep under review the potential impact of the Government's proposal to withdraw regional development grants and other forms of regional assistance from Shetland, Orkney and Nairn, as part of plans to reduce the areas eligible for such assistance by 1982. Economic conditions in these areas could change dramatically within a few years, and the board attach considerable importance to the review of the proposals promised in 1982 before eligibility for all forms of assistance is removed. One of the important implications of de-scheduling these areas for UK regional policy is that they would also be ineligible for assistance from the European Regional Development Fund. The Scottish Economic Planning Department have commissioned a research project, in which board staff have co-operated, to assess prospects for these areas and the inner Moray Firth which will take special account of the impact of the oil sector.

20 The board were invited to submit written evidence to the House of Lords European Communities Committee on their inquiry into EEC regional policy, with special reference to the operation of the European Regional Development Fund (ERDF). In evidence, the board welcomed a stronger and more effective regional policy in the community which can only be of benefit to a peripheral area like the Highlands and

Islands and argued for closer links with the fund authorities and their more direct involvement with regional problems. The main conclusion of the evidence was that the operation of the ERDF is restricted by a number of factors, in particular the principle of additionality, which limit the incentive for a regional agency such as the board to press actively for ERDF assistance. The board put forward two proposals — the retrospective refund of board discretionary assistance to projects from ERDF, thereby maintaining the budget available to the board for assisting other projects, or the board to receive a supplementary budget from the community. In our evidence, we stated our preference for the second proposal for a supplementary budget.

21 During the year we had a number of direct contacts with the EEC. Although the integrated development programme (IDP) for the Western Isles had still not been ratified by the community, we co-operated with DAFS, the Western Isles Islands Council, and the Crofters Commission in setting up a steering committee and working parties to prepare detailed proposals for the IDP.

Policy and development research

Ferry services

22 In February 1980 the Scottish Office issued a consultative paper 'Sea Transport to the Scottish Islands' which discussed a number of options relating to the introduction of a form of Road Equivalent Tariff (RET). Because of our historical association with the introduction of the concept, the board were among the first to comment on the paper. We expressed disappointment with the lack of development of ideas we put forward as early as 1974, since when many circumstances have changed. Nevertheless, we welcomed the Government's interest in RET and concluded that, despite the problems raised in the consultative paper, there were no insuperable obstacles to the introduction of RET.

23 We proposed that the ultimate objective should be a tariff related to the running costs of vehicles, excluding the costs of depreciation, licensing and insurance. The main obstacle to such a basis would be the additional subsidy required, which we estimate would rise from the 1980 level of around £5 million to £15 million. The scheme could, however, be introduced in stages to reduce the immediate impact of such a steep increase. We welcomed the suggestion of a route licensing system which, we believe, could be arranged so as to offer incentives to operators to lower costs while ensuring an adequate standard of service.

24 In May we published Transport Research Paper 6, 'The Future of Ferry Services in the Highlands and Islands', which set out ideas for restructuring Scottish vehicle ferry services over the next twenty years. The principal suggestions were for a number of shorter ferry routes, the attainment of capacity by increased frequency of services rather than by size of vessel alone, the gradual introduction of a standard fleet of interchangeable ships on all but the longest routes, improvements in the control and reporting of the ferry system and the introduction of RET as soon as practicable. The paper was not a plan or programme but was intended to stimulate thought and discussion on the optimum form of future vehicle ferry services and complemented our response on RET. It is the board's belief that re-structuring will be essential if an equitable fare structure is to be introduced and the consequent operating subsidy maintained at a level acceptable to Government.

The Orkney ferry St Ola docks at Scrabster, Caithness.

Prices and transport

25 For many years the board have been concerned at the relatively high prices for some foods, consumer goods and bulk materials in islands and the extent to which those prices may be attributed to transport costs. Aspects of this problem have been investigated in several research projects commissioned or conducted by the board. These include freight rates and prices, alternative fare structures (RET), the establishment of local price indices and patterns of expenditure. To follow up that research we commissioned a study to examine more fully the whole distribution system for goods, including costs other than transport, such as warehousing, inventory costs, handling charges in breaking bulk and overheads. A number of distribution 'chains' are being examined in detail — Glasgow-Oban-Tiree/Coll-Barra, Glasgow-Inverness-Ullapool-Stornoway-Ness and Aberdeen/Inverness-Stromness-Kirkwall-North Isles. The objective is to clarify the extent to which the cost of goods on islands is raised by factors other than ferry charges and the transport difficulties of remote areas other than islands. A report is expected during the latter half of 1981.

Rural prices survey

26 The Institute for the Study of Sparsely Populated Areas at Aberdeen University again carried out four prices surveys

on behalf of the board and the Scottish Consumer Council. The prices of goods in local shops were collected by volunteers and local authorities; other items making up the cost of living, such as housing and transport, were estimated by the institute. The surveys have confirmed earlier conclusions that prices are higher in most rural areas than in Scottish towns and cities. The differential between the average rural location and Aberdeen is around 10% while the highest variance, to be found on small remote islands, is closer to 20%. It is hoped that these surveys will be financed in future by a wider range of interested bodies. The board have also maintained an interest in the study on consumers in remote areas commissioned and funded by the Scottish Consumer Council and being carried out by the Institute for the Study of Sparsely Populated Areas.

Pulp mill closure

27 The threat to the Lochaber area arising from the closure of the pulp mill and the board's programmes to introduce new employment are described in paragraphs 63 to 65. Two research studies were carried out to assess the wider implications of closure for migration and for related industries. To assess the probable reactions of redundant workers and their families, we interviewed workers to establish a profile of the available labour force. The results showed that the great majority of workers intended to seek other employment opportunities in the area and, indeed, had every reason to do so since most had families and dependants either working or being educated locally.

28 The closure represented a threat to a much wider area in the Highlands from disruption of timber harvesting, transport and other service employment. A report was commissioned from the Scottish Council Research Institute (SCRI) who had previously carried out a study of the economic prospects of Lochaber and research on input-output links within Scottish industry. Their conclusions were that in the short term (less than five years) the alternative outlets for small roundwood and sawmill residues were likely to take up quantities similar to the pulp mill. Indeed, the scale of timber exports to Scandinavia had, by the end of the year, begun to exceed the quantities consumed at Corpach. In the long term, however, this demand is uncertain and after 1986 there is likely to be an increase in the availability of small roundwood in the Forestry Commission's North of Scotland Conservancy. The board are now considering the recommendations of the report and of ways to assist areas in Mull, Kintyre and Ardnamurchan which may not be able to participate in the current export of timber through east coast ports.

New technology

29 PA Management Consultants reported during the year on their study for the board on the impact of micro-electronics technology on the Highlands and Islands. The study was intended to identify possible new business opportunities for, and threats to, existing businesses in the area, and the possibilities of attracting new businesses based on this

technology. The principal conclusions of the study on existing industry in the board's area, based on an interview survey, were that awareness of new technology in the area is very low and that there is significant potential for the application of micro-electronics in key sectors. The board have accepted the recommendation that we should stimulate awareness through the Department of Industry's scheme, MAPCON. Opportunities for the application of micro-electronics technology appear to be present to a greater extent in improvements to production and other processes than for the development of products based on micro-electronic components. Correspondingly, threats to the local economy from outside competition in the form of new products are thought to be low but of significance in some sectors. The report also identified specific inward investment opportunities and compared alternative strategies to attract new ventures, the main features of which will be incorporated into the programme proposed by the board's industrial development and marketing division.

30 The rapid strides in the development of information technology could have very important implications for peripheral areas, and we are maintaining contact with a number of projects and agencies in this field. More immediately the board have during 1980 become an information provider on Prestel, the British Telecommunications public viewdata service. The HIDB database is now on Prestel 44570. We are the most northerly information provider in the UK and, to date, the most northerly user. As well as providing general information about the structure and activities of the board the database contains sections on assistance for development and tourism. The information is cross-linked with the Prestel databases of the Scottish Development Agency and the Scottish Tourist Board.

31 In the field of advanced technology, we have applied the use of satellite imagery to the problems of surveying the board's large area of land and sea. In this way we can take advantage, at low cost, of the massive investment undertaken for scientific and strategic purposes mainly by the USA. In a large, rugged area such as the Highlands and Islands, the benefits of widely available, small-scale photography are of increasing importance since land use and other data obtained by conventional air photography are difficult to organise and very expensive when applied to large areas. Photography or, more accurately, electronic imagery from space satellites is rapidly improving in quality and availability. We have started three projects which will produce data on marine conditions related to fisheries, snow cover in winter sports areas over the period of the seventies, and primary uses of land throughout the board's area. To give an indication of the potential of remote sensing, the land use studies are aimed at data accurate to within 30 metres — accuracy that will improve as techniques develop. Much of this work will be completed during 1981.

Community co-operatives

32 1980 was the third full year of the board's community co-operative scheme. By March, we were sufficiently encouraged by progress to extend the duration of the scheme for a further three years. At the end of the year 34 activities with 22 full-time, 61 part-time and 13 seasonal employees were generating an annual community co-operative turnover of some £500,000. On this basis the rate of development of these locally controlled multi-functional enterprises, once operational, has been rather better than originally projected, though it is still too early to assess profitability.

33 Three new community co-operatives were registered in 1980, bringing the total to ten of which seven are operational. Eight are in the Western Isles, one in Orkney and one on the west Highland mainland. Two steering committees are planning further community co-ops and a number of other groups have expressed interest. The table on page 20 shows the various activities being undertaken and projected by each co-op. Of these, the exhibition, tearoom and craft shop operated by Co-chomunn na Hearadh illustrates the ability of a community co-op to manage a board project for local benefit — in this case the 'An Clachan' craft complex at Leverburgh.

34 There has been an encouraging tendency for contact and co-operation between community co-ops. During the year assemblies of community co-op representatives took place in Iochdar and in Ness. A recent development is a proposed joint approach by Co-Chomuinn nan Eilean (Western Isles Community Co-ops) to the EEC for funding towards the cost of co-op projects under the integrated development programme proposed for the Western Isles. The need for effective training is a matter of growing importance to all community co-operatives and the board are placing emphasis on appropriate training and guidance programmes for community co-op personnel.

35 Interest continues to be expressed in the community co-op scheme locally, nationally and internationally, and there appears to be an increasing recognition that the community co-operative concept is a development option worthy of consideration. Formal links between community co-operatives and the co-operative movement as a whole strengthened in the course of the year with fishermen's craft and agricultural co-operatives and with the Co-operative Wholesale Society Ltd. We are encouraged by this trend. The link with the CWS in particular has proved to be of practical value to the three community co-operatives operating shops.

36 The community development approach reflected in the co-operative scheme has been promoted on other fronts. We have maintained contact with a variety of groups and individuals with a view to improving local information and

COMMUNITY CO-OPERATIVES 1980

Category	Enterprises	Ness	Vatersay	Eriskay (1)	Park	Papa Westray	Harris (2)	Iochdar	Scalpay	Barra (3)	Teachd ar Tir
Land	Horticulture	•	×				•	•			•
	Agricultural Plant Hire	•			•					×	
	Agricultural Requisites	•			•	•		×		×	
	Peat Cutting				•						
	Livestock Rearing		•							×	
Sea & Fish	Fish Farming				•						
	Fish Processing			×					×		
	Fishermen's Requisites			×			•			×	
	Lobster Holding									×	
Building & Manufacturing	Building Contracting	•									
	Building Supplies	×					×	×			
	Plant Hire		×		•					×	
	Manufacturing Workshop	×					×				×
	Knitwear			•	•		×				
	Sheepskin Curing				×			×			
	Craft Marketing					•	•	•			•
	Bakery						×	×			
Services & Tourism	Museum/Cultural Centre						•				•
	Hostel/Guest House					×					
	Package Tours					•					
	Self-catering Cottages			×		×					
	Garage	×									×
	Retail Shop	•	•	•		•	•				
	Catering	•	×			•	•	•	×	•	
	Community Hall							•			
	Community Mini Bus							•			
	Coal/Fuel	•		×			•		×		

× Projected • In operation

Footnote:

(1) includes activities of Eriskay Fishermen's Co-op Ltd.

(2) includes activities of Harris Craft Guild and Harris Fishermen's Co-op Ltd.

(3) includes activities of Barra Fishermen's Co-op Ltd.

fostering development. In north and west Sutherland, one of the most economically depressed parts of the board's area, a special project has been launched to raise the level and effectiveness of assistance. We have appointed a field officer in the area, initially for three years, to encourage community and individual initiatives at local level. We have given financial assistance to a voluntary development group in Assynt to investigate local potential.

Social development

37 In 1980, the board were able to help 140 social development schemes with finance of £314,000. Over the past four years the number of social projects which have been assisted has risen from 62 in 1976 to 140 in 1980. Our budget for social

Community co-operatives
as at December 1980
Committee formed
Co-operative formed
Papa Westray
Eday
Hoy
Ness
Great Bernera
Park
Scalpay
Harris
Iochdar
Eriskay
Acharacle

development has nearly trebled in the corresponding period, an indication of the importance which we attach to helping local communities improve the quality of life in the Highlands and Islands. In most cases our assistance matches the contribution by a local voluntary organisation towards the shortfall in funding a project, after grant aid by local authorities and central government agencies has been taken into account. In many schemes, however, the board are the only source of financial assistance and in these cases we are ready to encourage self-help by local organisations through grant aid on a £ for £ basis.

38 Of the schemes assisted in 1980, almost one-third were for village halls, either for building works or furnishings and equipment. Others included sports facilities and equipment, community TV schemes, environmental improvements, cultural events, and projects initiated by community councils.

39 The social development programme encourages initiative and enterprise by local people in providing facilities for community use which help create a more stable and contented environment. This is particularly true of remote areas where there are few opportunities available for social, recreational and educational activities, for which a village hall is normally vital. The board were, therefore, concerned to learn that the capital grants scheme for youth, village hall and community centre projects, administered by the Scottish Education Department and local authorities under the Further Education (Scotland) Regulations 1959, was under review by the Secretary of State.

40 There was a distinct possibility that in future, as had already been decided in England, the scheme might be replaced by additional rate support grant to local authorities. If a similar arrangement is adopted in Scotland, and since rate support grant is unlikely to include a specific allocation for halls and community centres, there could be no guarantee that the extra sum given to local authorities would be used for halls and community centres. The board decided, therefore, to submit representations through the Minister of State that the capital grants scheme should be retained in its present form. We can see no administrative burden in continuing the scheme as it stands, but if any such problem does exist we are willing to play a part in administering the scheme within the Highlands and Islands.

41 One aspect of social development which we have kept under constant review is the growth of radio and television broadcasting within the Highlands and Islands. We have helped several isolated communities to install cable distribution systems from a communal aerial, enabling householders in such areas to receive television signals. An added problem is that the 405-line VHF television service is being phased out and replaced by the 625-line UHF system. Although the British Broadcasting Corporation and the

TV coverage

as at December 1980

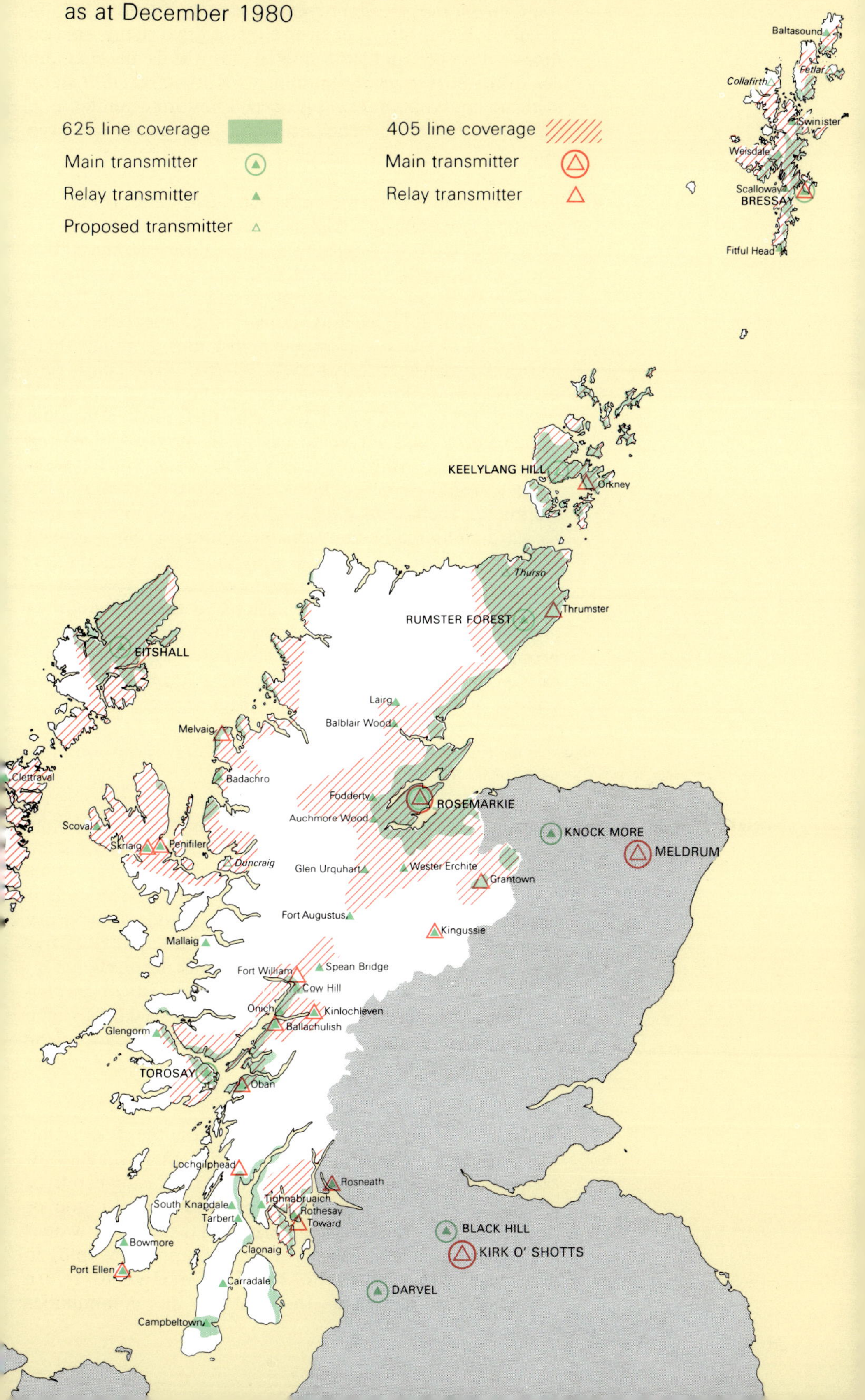
625 line coverage
Main transmitter
Relay transmitter
Proposed transmitter
405 line coverage
Main transmitter
Relay transmitter
Baltasound
Fetlar
Collafirth
Swinister
Weisdale
Scalloway
BRESSAY
Fitful Head
KEELYLANG HILL
Orkney
Thurso
Thrumster
RUMSTER FOREST
EITSHALL
Lairg
Balblair Wood
Melvaig
Badachro
Clettraval
Fodderty
ROSEMARKIE
Auchmore Wood
KNOCK MORE
MELDRUM
Scoval
Skriaig
Penifiler
Duncraig
Glen Urquhart
Wester Erchite
Grantown
Fort Augustus
Kingussie
Mallaig
Fort William
Spean Bridge
Cow Hill
Onich
Kinlochleven
Ballachulish
Glengorm
TOROSAY
Oban
Lochgilphead
Rosneath
South Knapdale
Tighnabruaich
Tarbert
Rothesay
Toward
BLACK HILL
Bowmore
Claonaig
KIRK O' SHOTTS
Port Ellen
Carradale
DARVEL
Campbeltown

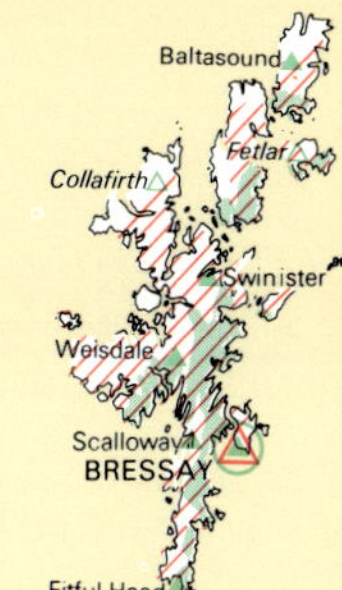

Independent Broadcasting Authority are constantly extending their services to small communities by the introduction of new transmitters, it is known that a great many isolated areas within the Highlands and Islands will not benefit from the overall coverage of the country for some years. In many such areas it is not practicable or economic for a community, under a self-help scheme, to install a cable distribution system.

42 For some time the Home Office have had under review the question of allowing small isolated communities to erect their own relay transmitting system, under Home Office licence, to serve householders in remote communities. During the year we made representations to the Home Office stressing the need to adopt a more lenient attitude to the issuing of licences to small communities, to enable them to install a self-help relay system where this was considered the most practicable and economic method of obtaining TV signals. We were pleased to learn subsequently that the Home Office had agreed to new procedures for licensing groups in areas which are too small and isolated to benefit from national coverage, but were anxious to erect a relay station at their own expense. This is a significant step forward and already many small communities have applied to the board for assistance in providing relay systems.

43 We have also made representations to the Home Office about the special fee of £100 for a relay licence which small groups have to meet over and above the normal cost of a television licence. We believe this to be an imposition on a section of the community, who, because of geographical location, are unable to obtain a national broadcasting service readily available to people resident in more populous areas.

Social research

44 The two-year fellowship on migration studies funded by the board in the Institute for the Study of Sparsely Populated Areas at Aberdeen University expired in January 1980 and a final report was issued by the institute in May. The study is based on information gathered during periods of residence in seven areas in Caithness, Lochaber, Sutherland, Orkney and the Western Isles. The communities were chosen to represent a wide range of areas and characteristics typical of smaller communities in the Highlands and Islands which had suffered from a declining or static population in the 1970's. The report 'Migration in the Highlands and Islands of Scotland' is available from the institute.

45 An important general point to emerge from the study is that the majority of people migrate from their locality or community at some stage in their life. The objective of development in an area, therefore, cannot be to stop or discourage emigration but to ensure that the outflow does not have damaging effects on the communities and, in particular, allows them to remain attractive to return migration or incomers. In most of the communities

surveyed, emigration is now much more balanced by inflows of population, reflecting the improved demographic trends in the area. In some areas the researcher detected a possibly important change in the attitude of young people, as compared to the older generation, that they are quick to take up opportunities locally when they arise. The major determinant of migration is the availability of employment opportunities, but in a number of areas, particularly in Caithness and Lochaber, the availability of housing has been an important attraction. A tentative conclusion is drawn that, in future, housing shortage may become a relatively greater constraint on development as more young people wish to stay and others to return.

46 We have maintained contact with a number of research projects. The head of our social development section has continued to act as an assessor to the North Sea Oil Panel of the Social Science Research Council, which has financed a number of studies on social aspects of oil-related development. We have commissioned work from the Department of Geography at Dundee University to test the feasibility of developing social indicators to complement the economic data at present the principal basis of policy decisions in Highlands and Islands development.

47 Education figures significantly in other studies with which the board are connected, for example a project by the Organisation for Economic Co-operation and Development on education and local development described in paragraph 115, and a study of rural primary school organisation by Aberdeen University, financed by the Scottish Education Department. Of particular interest is a projected two-year course in cultural and practical studies planned by the Gaelic College at Sabhal Mor Ostaig, which we have agreed to part-finance for an initial period.

Transport policy and research

48 The board welcomed the decision of Scottish Office to assume responsibility for, and increase, the subsidy to Highlands and Islands airports operated by the Civil Aviation Authority. Otherwise the stated intention of the CAA to make the airports break even would have led to a level of charges which would seriously discourage both business and social travel by air. Following consultation with the board, the CAA have begun to establish consultative committees on the operation of local airports in the Highlands and Islands. We will be represented on each committee and have already attended inaugural meetings in Inverness and Wick. Following a preliminary meeting it was decided that a committee is not required for Kirkwall airport.

49 The winter week survey of the origin and destination of passengers using Inverness airport was mounted in February. Despite the diversion of several flights because of fog in the middle part of the week, satisfactory samples of passengers were achieved. The results were subsequently

analysed and published as HIDB Transport Research Paper 7, 'Inverness Air Passenger Survey 1979-80'. This report was circulated to the CAA, airline operators and other interested parties, and generated several inquiries for more detailed data on traffic between Inverness and Europe. In discussions with the airlines, it emerged that one international scheduled service is being considered for operation when the currently depressed air travel market picks up again. New domestic air services to and from Inverness, providing better overseas connections, are also being investigated.

50 The board have received the final report of the consultants examining the potential for a freightliner terminal in Inverness. The report, which was commissioned in conjunction with Highland Regional Council, British Rail and Freightliner Ltd, states that there is insufficient demand for a full terminal but that a facility based on loading by mobile crane could be viable. It is understood that Freightliner Ltd are now examining ways in which such a terminal could be managed.

51 We helped the councils of social service in East Ross and Black Isle and North and West Sutherland to retain transport specialists in the University of Aberdeen to examine public transport in their respective areas. The studies will look at the availability of public transport and relate it to the distribution of retail, health and education facilities, and identify the ease of access for the public to those facilities and the degree of dependence of settlements on public transport. Recommendations for improved coordination and low cost changes to the public transport system will be made. Reports are expected during 1981.

Petrol supplies

52 Early in the year the board circulated every petrol retailing site in the Highlands and Islands with a questionnaire designed to achieve two purposes, to help determine the threat of closure in the near future and to obtain data on facilities for a tourist map. Responses to questions about the age of equipment and current viability suggested that pressure on the low turnover supplier would remain strong. Consequently, we are considering ways in which we might support the continuation of supplies in areas where the only local outlet is under closure threat. The petrol stations map published early in the tourist season shows the location of the area's petrol stations, opening times, breakdown and emergency facilities and diesel suppliers. The map has been distributed through tourist information offices to holiday motorists.

Air surveys

53 We commissioned eleven air photographic surveys to meet the needs of the development divisions. Because of adverse weather conditions during the summer it was only possible to complete those for Breasclete, Wick and environs and Loch Gunna (Lewis). Limited coverage was obtained for Nigg Bay. In addition, oblique colour photographs were taken of the north face of the Cairngorms, the Spey Valley

and parts of the Cromarty Firth. Some of the photography was used in the preparation of vertical mosaics.

Energy

54 In addition to sponsoring our own conference on energy, on which we report in paragraphs 61 and 62, the board have maintained an interest in alternative methods of energy production and use which reduce the cost of living and production in the HIDB area. Staff contributed two papers to the conference on 'Energy for Remote and Island Communities' held in September at Eden Court Theatre, Inverness. While most research and development in this field is funded at a national level by scientific and technological agencies, the board have joined with the Scottish Development Agency in contributing to the cost of a research and development project on biomass energy sources being conducted under the European Economic Community's FAST programme (Forecasting and Assessment in Science and Technology). The project will examine the contribution of biomass to overall energy supplies and the potential for development of this form of energy in Scotland. The board's principal interest is in the possible use of land in the Highlands for biomass 'crops' and as sites of generation, together with the possibility of smaller-scale direct applications of the technology in the area. The project began in November and will be completed within twelve months.

Eden Court Theatre

55 In view of the steadily deteriorating financial position of the Eden Court Theatre, the board agreed to a request by the theatre's governors to finance a study on the future viability of the theatre at a cost of £10,000. This included an assessment of the contribution of the theatre to the area and how it could be enhanced, and the operation and financing of the theatre. The board were represented on the committee which monitored the study, completed in October. The report's recommendations on management and financial control and projections of future financial needs have provided a basis for discussions on broadening the base of support for the theatre from local authorities and the Scottish Arts Council.

Population Distribution

Settlement populations (1971)

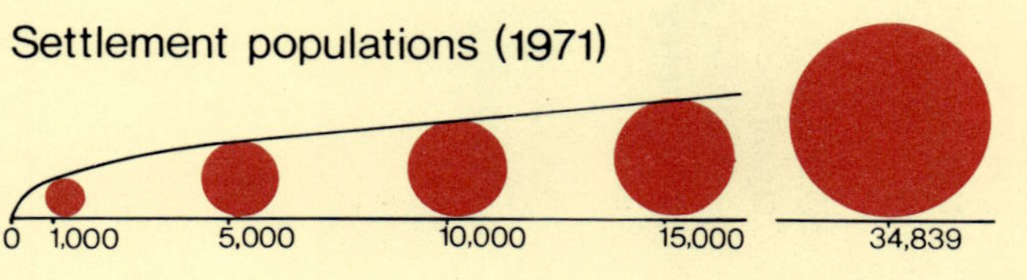

Dispersed population (1961)

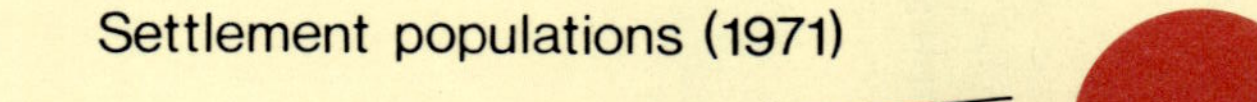

Based on a map researched by Miss M Gordon and Mrs I Robertson and produced by the University of Glasgow

Region or Islands area

District

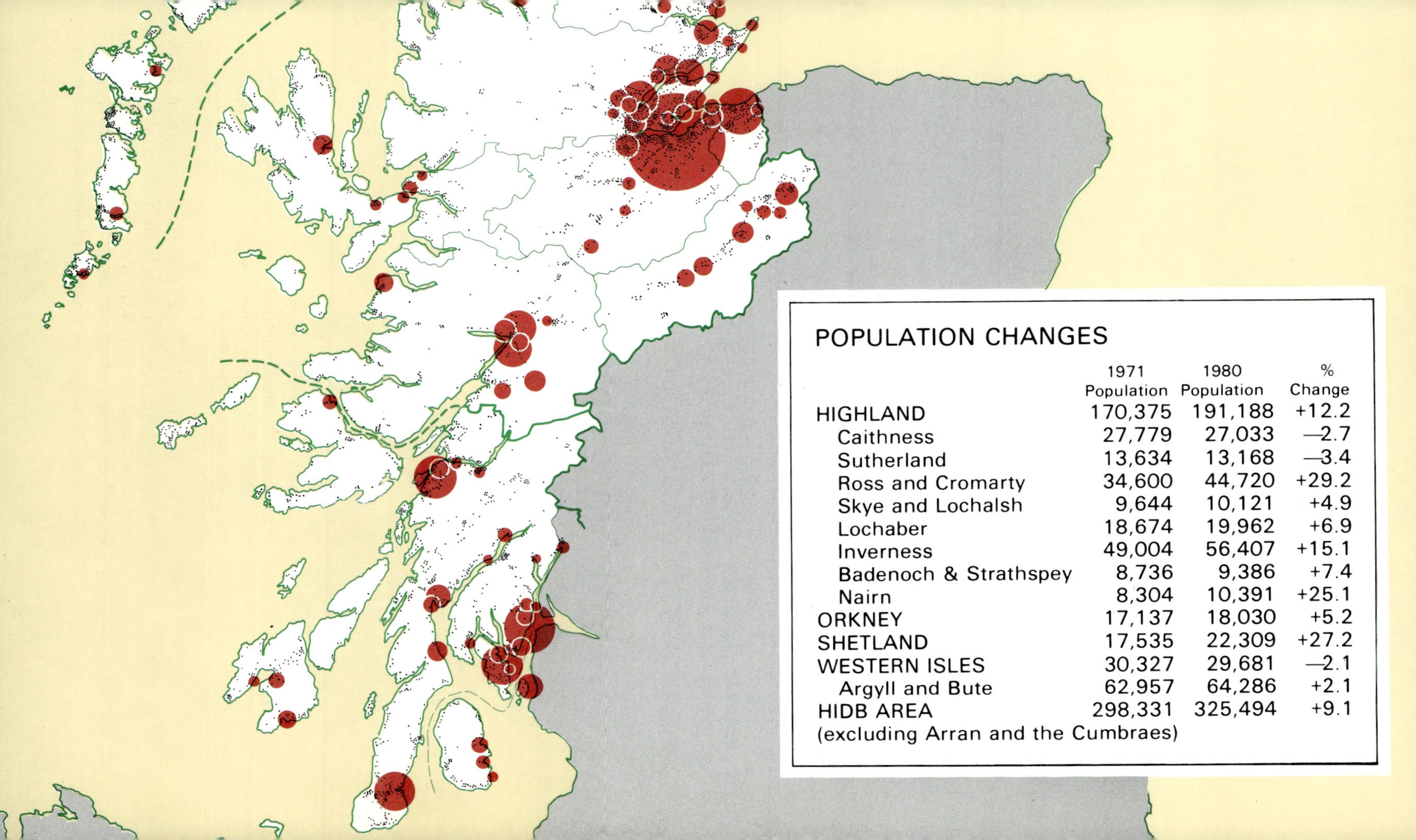

POPULATION CHANGES

	1971 Population	1980 Population	% Change
HIGHLAND	170,375	191,188	+12.2
Caithness	27,779	27,033	—2.7
Sutherland	13,634	13,168	—3.4
Ross and Cromarty	34,600	44,720	+29.2
Skye and Lochalsh	9,644	10,121	+4.9
Lochaber	18,674	19,962	+6.9
Inverness	49,004	56,407	+15.1
Badenoch & Strathspey	8,736	9,386	+7.4
Nairn	8,304	10,391	+25.1
ORKNEY	17,137	18,030	+5.2
SHETLAND	17,535	22,309	+27.2
WESTERN ISLES	30,327	29,681	—2.1
Argyll and Bute	62,957	64,286	+2.1
HIDB AREA (excluding Arran and the Cumbraes)	298,331	325,494	+9.1

Industry, marketing and transport

Highlights

56 Although the level of general industrial investment in the Highlands and Islands in 1980 was a little subdued by comparison with preceding years, the reduction in the number of industrial projects was less than might have been feared. On the whole industry in the area stood up reasonably well to the recession, but many markets and industrial sectors were depressed to varying degrees and there was an abnormally high casualty rate among manufacturing and crafts firms.

57 The biggest casualty of all was the pulp mill at Corpach, by Fort William, which closed in November with the loss of about 460 jobs. This was a bitter blow for Lochaber, and earlier hopes that future employment could be safeguarded by a newsprint manufacturing project collapsed. It was clear that urgent action on our part was required to help restore the economic prosperity and self-confidence of the Fort William area. We gave the problem the highest priority and by the end of the year had implemented a comprehensive array of counter-measures described in detail in paragraphs 63 to 65.

58 The most encouraging single item of industrial news for the Highlands in 1980 came towards the end of the year, when Mr David Howell, Secretary of State for Energy, announced the Government's decision to authorise the construction of a major new gas-gathering pipeline system in the North Sea. The system will bring a mixture of natural gas and natural gas liquids ashore at St Fergus in Grampian Region, and a separate pipeline will be laid to transport some of the natural gas liquids to Nigg Bay on the Cromarty Firth. The availability of these materials will provide a basis for petrochemical manufacturing activities in the Cromarty Firth area, and greatly enhances the prospects of this type of development in the 1980's.

59 The board devoted a great deal of effort during 1980 to preparations for new measures in the industrial promotion field to be carried out in 1981. We decided to engage Venture Founders Corporation, a small but highly specialised American firm, to carry out a major exercise for us in

Scotland. This firm has a unique approach to finding and helping entrepreneurs to set up new businesses, and a remarkably successful record. The Bank of Scotland and the Industrial and Commercial Finance Corporation agreed to join the board in helping finance any promising new projects which emerge from the work of Venture Founders.

60 Plans were also completed for a promotional campaign aimed at about 800 companies engaged in the electronics and allied industries in the eastern United States. These companies were individually identified for us by El Tronics International Inc, a specialised consultancy firm located in Rockport, Massachusetts, who also advised on the preparation of promotional leaflets and on the general approach to be adopted in the campaign. A trial 'mail-shot' to 40 companies took place in September, but the principal campaign was timed to start in January 1981.

61 In collaboration with the Royal Society of Edinburgh, we sponsored a major conference on the theme 'Energy in the 90s' at the Aviemore Centre in October. The proceedings attracted about 80 delegates and were opened by Mr Alex Fletcher, MP, Parliamentary Under Secretary of State at the Scottish Office. Mr Hamish Gray, MP, Minister of State at the Department of Energy, spoke after the formal conference dinner.

62 The principal objective for the board was to draw attention to the important contribution which the Highlands and Islands, including the adjacent sea areas, are capable of making to the UK's energy needs in the nineties and beyond. The Royal Society were particularly interested to explore some of the scientific and technical problems which have to be resolved in the development of new sources of energy. The papers produced a wide-ranging and lively discussion and received considerable publicity, particularly for the impressive assessment of the future of the Scottish offshore oil industry by Mr John Raisman, chairman and chief executive of Shell UK Limited. Sir Kenneth Blaxter, president of the Royal Society of Edinburgh, contributed a masterly summing-up and undertook the task of editing the proceedings for publication. The conference raised a number of issues pertinent to regional development which we will follow up in the future.

Special measures

63 Following news of the decision to close the pulp mill at Corpach in November, we commissioned preliminary assessments of the potential for stimulating alternative forms of development in the area from two firms, Job Creation Ltd and Coopers & Lybrand Associates. In parallel with these, our staff interviewed 197 of the people faced with redundancy to determine the skills and job experience which would be available for new employers, and the future aspirations of the individuals concerned. This indicated a widespread desire to remain in the area. It was followed by a short seminar and individual interviews for a

number of people who were interested in starting small businesses of their own. Special priority was given to accelerating our industrial building and site acquisition programme in the Fort William area.

64 In November we announced a two pronged attempt to reverse rising unemployment in Lochaber. The first part of this involves the setting up of a small local team by Job Creation Ltd to stimulate the growth of local businesses, using the experience and techniques built up in other areas where major industrial closures have taken place. It is planned that this team will work in Fort William under the board's aegis for about three years. Job Creation Ltd also hope to persuade some outside firms to locate new investments in the Fort William area. The second part of the programme involves screening about 2,000 firms in the USA as potential incomers to the area. This work is being undertaken by Coopers & Lybrand, who have access to a network of more than 80 offices across North America. Their intensive search for US companies ripe for expansion on this side of the Atlantic will concentrate mainly on the fields of fine chemicals and pharmaceuticals, electronics and related equipment, and possibly off-shore oil equipment.

65 We also maintained contact with the Scottish Economic Planning Department and commercial interests in discussing possible new timber-using industries for the Fort William area.

Light industry

66 We approved financial assistance for 58 light manufacturing and craft ventures in 1980. Total board investment was £1.5 million complemented by £2.3 million from private and other public sources. These ventures were expected to produce 298 jobs in the course of the next few years. The largest completely new business to be supported will manufacture electronic circuits in a custom-built factory now under construction for the board at Rothesay. Another new electronics venture is being set up in one of our advance factories at Sandbank, Dunoon, to produce security systems. We are assisting two new sawmilling projects, at Alness and Muir of Ord, and a new business building bodies for commercial motor vehicles which has been set up in Inverness in a vacant board factory extended to accommodate the venture. A vacant advance workshop at Lochgilphead was leased for use as a ceramics production unit and a new business producing high-quality pine furniture opened in Fort William.

67 Among existing businesses, one of the largest and most important projects we assisted during the year was the extensive modernisation and re-equipment of the Kilmallie sawmill at Fort William, which is also being partly funded by the Scottish Development Agency. This investment is expected to secure a substantial number of jobs on a long-term basis, both in the sawmill and in associated timber harvesting and transportation activities. Other large invest-

ment projects for which we approved assistance included the installation of modern cheese-making equipment in a creamery in Argyll, additional working capital for an oil-related business in Caithness, and the expansion of a quarry in Ross-shire.

68 In Shetland we gave further support to the knitwear industry, and we were particularly pleased to assist with the commercial development of a local spinning mill following the satisfactory outcome of extended trials with the spinning of local wool. Orcadian businesses to receive help for expansion included a manufacturing bakery. The market for Harris Tweed continued to be buoyant, and we helped to fund the second stage of a scheme for purchasing new looms for weavers. It was also agreed to proceed with a 10,000 square feet extension to a wool mill in Stornoway occupied by one of the principal Harris Tweed manufacturers.

69 Projects assisted in the Highland Region included the relocation and expansion of a business specialising in the disposal and reprocessing of industrial wastes, the installation of a milk pasteurising plant, and expansion by a confectionery manufacturer. In Argyll and Bute District we helped expand an engineering business in Mull, and assisted food processing businesses in Campbeltown and Dunoon and a textile manufacturer in Bute.

70 Many manufacturing firms found 1980 a difficult year, with depressed market conditions — sometimes exacerbated by new competition from overseas — and high interest rates. In this situation selective financial assistance to retain employment in firms with sound long-term prospects assumed greater importance. While we were able to help in several cases, a substantial number of board-assisted businesses were forced to close, or were run down to a very low level of activity. These included several knitwear businesses in the Western Isles, a pottery in Sandbank (Argyll), and an adhesive tape manufacturer in Dingwall. In addition, Alginate Industries shut two of their three seaweed processing factories in the Western Isles, J Arthur Dixon decided to close their Inverness printing factory in a group rationalisation plan, and another printing project in Inverness was abandoned because of failure to resolve problems between the company and the print union concerned.

Service industry

71 In the service industry sector, help was approved for 75 projects. The total sum committed by the board was £800,000. The largest single project was the establishment of a caravan servicing and repair facility at Nairn, but many of the cases involved local services in remote rural areas and the smaller islands, such as building trades, agricultural engineering, electrical repairs, garages and a few isolated shops. We helped several transport operators to acquire minibuses and a blacksmith to purchase equipment for a mobile agricultural repair service in Islay and Jura. A local

dry-cleaning service in Shetland qualified for assistance, as did a photographic processing unit and a specialised car tuning centre in Ross-shire.

72 Projects assisted in the Western Isles included purchase of a mobile snack-bar by the community co-operative at Ness in Lewis, and a new small passenger and freight boat for use on the Sound of Harris. We also approved financial assistance for the community co-operative at Iochdar (South Uist) to operate a building materials supply service if they were successful in their bid to purchase the Department of Agriculture and Fisheries' building materials store at Carnan. In support of local health facilities, we assisted a medical practice in Arran and a dental practice in East Sutherland.

Factories and industrial sites

73 We completed seven industrial building projects during the year which added 51,000 square feet to the area's factory and workshop facilities — a 5,000sqft factory extension for Britain's only ski manufacturer at Aviemore, an 18,000sqft factory extension for clothing production in Campbeltown, a 10,000sqft 'bespoke' factory for cast polyester resin art products in Lochgilphead, an 8,000sqft advance factory in twin units at Sandbank, Dunoon, a 5,000sqft factory for timber-frame house production in Skye, a 2,500sqft advance workshop in South Uist, and a 2,500sqft factory extension for confectionery manufacture in Stromness.

74 Tenants were found for vacant board properties at Wick, Golspie and Inverness. The 6,000sqft advance factory at Wick is being leased to a company manufacturing leather goods, who are transferring this operation from an old building on the Wick Airport Industrial Estate. Two of our small workshop units at Golspie are being used for the manufacture of creels and allied products, and two others are under construction for a printing industry venture. At Inverness, work began on a 4,000sqft extension to a factory leased to a thermostatic control manufacturer, and three of the four 'nest' units completed in 1979 were allocated to expanding printing and publishing firms and a car component distributor.

75 We decided to embark on a further programme of advance factories and workshops in order to take full advantage of future recovery in the investment climate, with particular emphasis on 'starter' units for small businesses. The new programme, which will cost over £3 million and includes advance factory and workshop projects previously approved but delayed, is shown on page 37 (buildings on which work had begun by the end of 1980 are marked with an asterisk).

76 In addition, we decided to purchase a number of prefabricated units which can be erected quickly to meet urgent needs for industrial or office premises and can be readily moved to other locations at a later date. These will be installed initially at Fort William, Ballachulish and Wick.

The 6,000sqft advance factory at Wick Airport leased to Caithness Leather Products.

Work began in 1980 on a 4,000sqft extension for Tarka Controls Ltd at Inverness.

The board's industrial estate at Golspie, Sutherland.

HIDB industrial properties

as at December 1980

Size of unit in square feet

- up to 4,999
- 5,000 to 9,999
- 10,000 to 19,999
- 20,000 and over

Each circle represents one factory unit

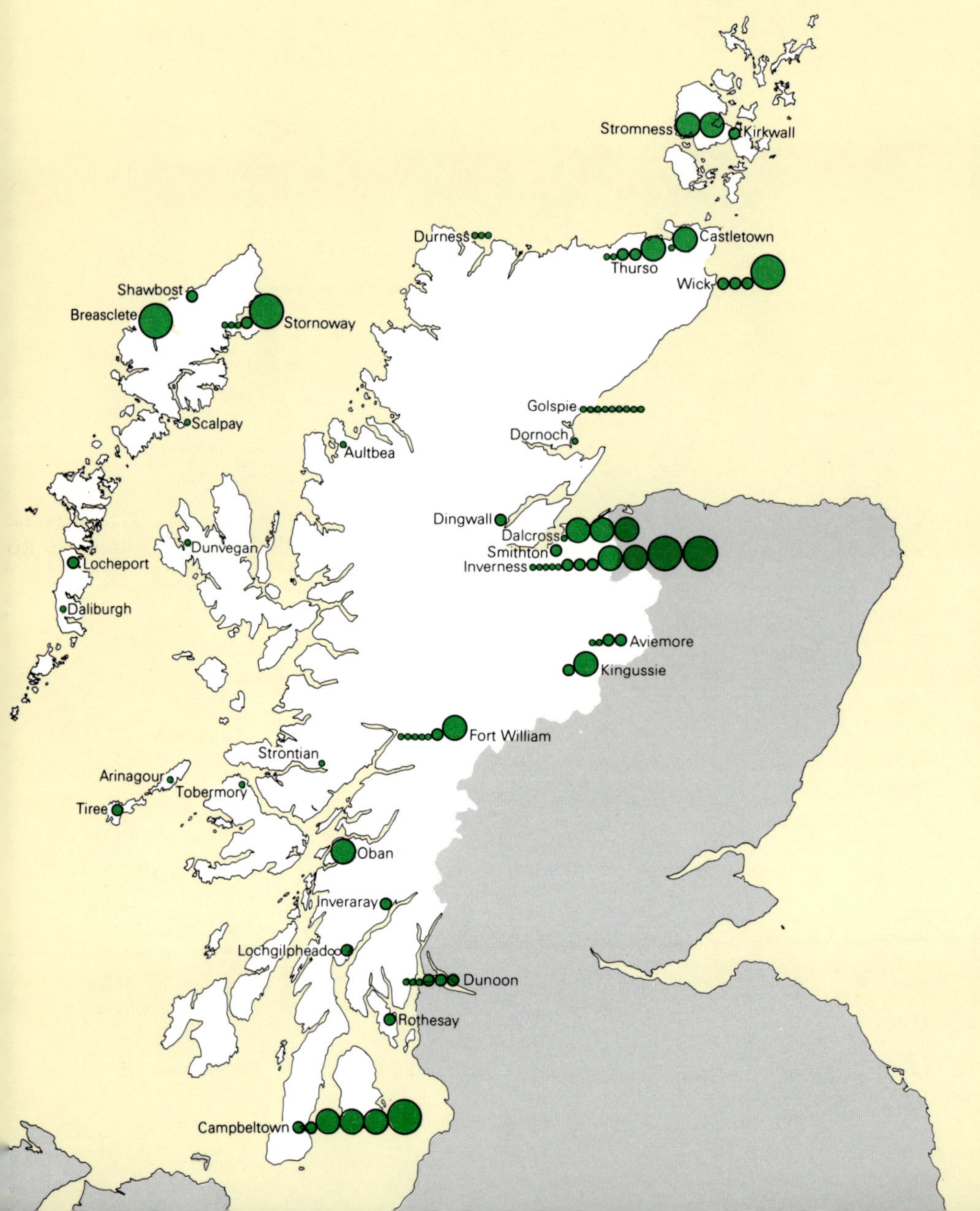

Location	*Buildings*
Kirkwall	2 x 2,000sq ft workshops
Lybster	2 x 750sq ft workshops
Helmsdale	2 x 1,200sq ft workshops
Brora	2,500sq ft workshop*
Golspie	2 x 750sq ft workshops*
Tain	2,000sq ft workshop
Alness	6,000sq ft factory
	2 x 750sq ft workshops
Ullapool	2,000sq ft workshop*
Muir of Ord	10,000sq ft factory*
Portree	2,500sq ft workshop
Inverness — Longman	6,000sq ft factory*
	2 x 1,500sq ft workshops
	2 x 750sq ft workshops
— Airport	5,000sq ft factory
Nairn	6,000sq ft factory*
	2 x 750sq ft workshops*
Grantown-on-Spey	3,300sq ft factory
Fort William	12,000sq ft factory*
	7,000sq ft group workshop units*
Ballachulish	2,000sq ft workshop
Mallaig	1,500sq ft workshop*
Strontian	Renovation of old school for crafts/light industry*
Tobermory	Renovation of existing factory
Lochgilphead	1,500sq ft workshop*
Islay	1,500sq ft workshop
Dunoon — Sandbank	2 x 750sq ft workshops
Tarbert (Argyll)	1,500sq ft workshop
Campbeltown	2 x 750sq ft workshops*
	8,000sq ft factory*
Tarbert (Harris)	1,500sq ft workshop

Sites for light industrial development were acquired at Kirkwall, Brora, Inverness (at the Longman Industrial Estate and the airport), Nairn, Grantown-on-Spey, Fort William, Caol, Mallaig and Campbeltown.

77 The staff of Highland Craftpoint, the new organisation set up by the board in partnership with the Scottish Development Agency to stimulate and support the development of the crafts industry in Scotland, moved into their new purpose-built complex at Beauly at the end of the year. Highland Craftpoint has taken over from the board the responsibility for providing individual advice to crafts firms on technical and marketing problems, and has instituted a wide range of short training courses as well as a crafts apprenticeship scheme. Other features of its activities will include demonstration workshops in ceramics and precious metals, a reference library, and exhibitions. The board nominate two members of Highland Craftpoint's management council and liaison arrangements at staff level are

Training courses are now underway at Highland Craftpoint's new headquarters at Beauly.

designed to co-ordinate activities between the two bodies. We retain responsibility for grants and loans towards the cost of setting up or expanding crafts businesses, and for providing rented workshops where appropriate.

Crafts

78 Many craft businesses encountered depressed market conditions in 1980, and several closed or cut back their operations. Even in this situation, however, there was still a trickle of new craft ventures whose proprietors were prepared to start on a modest scale. Financial assistance was approved for ten new crafts businesses including woodwork, pottery, weaving, wrought iron and metalwork, leatherwork, and the restoration of antique furniture and upholstery. We were especially pleased to be able to help a knitwear co-operative successfully organised and established by the people of Fair Isle.

79 The year saw some interesting developments in buildings devoted to craftwork. The new crafts complex and tearoom at Leverburgh, Harris — to be known as 'An Clachan' — was completed and leased to Co-Chomunn Na Hearadh, the Harris community co-operative. One of the features of the complex is an exhibition area, devoted mainly to the story of Harris Tweed and incorporating a loom to be used for weaving demonstrations. Design of the exhibition was undertaken by Highland Craftpoint, in consultation with the Harris Tweed Association, the community co-operative and the board. Apart from the tearoom and exhibition area, the complex incorporates a workshop and office, a retail shop, and storage accommodation. It is intended partly to serve as an added attraction to tourists, encouraging them to make a circular tour of Harris.

80 Following the renovation of the former railway station at Strathpeffer, carried out by the Scottish Development Agency on behalf of the Highland Regional Council, we agreed to take this attractive Victorian building on long

lease from the council. The building now provides accommodation for three small craft workshops, a tourist information office and an interpretive centre for the interest of tourists. We plan shortly to build two small craft workshops in the station area with a view to developing Strathpeffer as a focal point for various craft activities.

81 We also agreed to purchase from the Highland Regional Council the factory at Lochinver which is occupied by Highland Stoneware (Scotland) Ltd, and to construct a 2,500 square feet extension. The firm is to set up a second workshop and retail unit which we are now building for them at Ullapool.

Industrial promotion

82 After a slow start, the number of new industrial investment enquiries reaching us increased in the later part of the year. We placed a limited number of industrial promotion advertisements in the national and trade press during the year, as we felt that more extensive efforts would have brought little return in the subdued investment climate which pervaded most sectors of the economy.

83 The possibilities of attracting new electronics-related investment from the United States continued to engage our attention, and two of our senior staff visited the USA in October. The visit was timed to coincide with a presentation to local industrialists in Boston, sponsored by the Scottish Development Agency, at which the main speaker was Mr Alex Fletcher, MP, Parliamentary Under Secretary of State at the Scottish Office. While in the Boston area our representatives called on a number of companies with whom we have been in contact in the past and finalised with El Tronics International Inc details of the promotional campaign referred to in paragraph 60.

Oil, gas and petrochemicals

84 Throughout the year we continued to promote and encourage oil, gas and petrochemical developments at Nigg Bay. Considerable efforts were made to maintain close contact with potential commercial developers and the responsible departments of state and public corporations to ensure that the development potential of Nigg Bay was fully recognised.

85 Particular hopes rest upon the long-discussed North Sea gas gathering system. In early December we joined the Highland Regional Council and the Cromarty Firth Port Authority in a meeting with Mr David Howell, MP, Secretary of State for Energy, when we were able to present arguments, based on the national as well as the regional interest, for the development of Nigg Bay as one of the outlets for natural gas liquids coming ashore from the system. We therefore derived considerable encouragement from Mr Howell's subsequent announcement on the subject. He confirmed that the Government had approved the construction, by 1984, of a system to gather associated gas and natural gas liquids (NGL's) from oilfields in the British sector of the

North Sea. These resources will be piped to St Fergus, near Peterhead, where the methane gas will be fed into the British Gas grid. A pipeline will be laid to Nigg Bay to enable some of the NGL's (propane and butane) to be exported, while consideration will be given to the piping of ethane to companies for petrochemical development.

86 Strong interest in acquiring these NGL's has been expressed by companies with development proposals at Nigg Bay, Mossmorran, Peterhead, Grangemouth and Teeside. Two companies, Dow Chemicals and Highland Hydrocarbons, have advanced firm proposals for petrochemical development at Nigg Bay, to include NGL separation and the production of ethylene and other downstream products. There are good prospects that one or other of these companies will be able to secure sufficient NGL feedstock for their proposals to proceed. Such development would result in a major petrochemical complex at Nigg Bay, creating considerable employment and stimulating the economy of the entire inner Moray Firth area.

87 The British National Oil Corporation are proceeding on schedule to develop the inshore Beatrice field which lies just twelve miles from the coast of Sutherland, and oil production should start in the autumn of 1981. A 49-mile oil pipeline has been laid to Nigg Bay, where construction work on onshore installations is also proceeding satisfactorily. The marine terminal and storage facilities, which are expected to require some 110 direct employees, will be ready to receive and export oil when production starts. A marine supply base will also be completed at Invergordon.

88 A further ten blocks in the Moray Firth have been offered in the seventh round of North Sea licences, and it is understood that they have attracted considerable attention from oil companies. Licences will be awarded early in 1981, and it is expected that all of those in the Moray Firth will be taken up. This would ensure a high level of exploration activity in that area for the next few years, with prospects of further production activity both offshore and onshore.

An aerial mosaic of Nigg Bay (page 41) showing, bottom centre, the oil platform fabrication yard of Highlands Fabricators Ltd and, centre, the oil terminal being developed by the British National Oil Corporation to take oil from the Beatrice field. Reclamation planned for the area left of the oil terminal will provide the site for proposed petrochemical developments.

89 We have been actively involved with Highland Regional Council to promote the use of service facilities in Caithness to support exploration and production activities in the Moray Firth. The two bodies have formed a Caithness joint working party who have prepared promotional material and made contact with a number of oil companies known to be interested in the Moray Firth. Promotional activities will continue in 1981 in a substantial effort to bring more oil-related employment to Caithness.

90 In Shetland, the Sullom Voe oil terminal is approaching completion, and the construction force is already past its peak of around 7,000. By mid 1981 it is expected that this will have fallen by half. Whilst most of these construction

workers come from outside Shetland, it is estimated that over 800 local people are employed. As the operational staffing requirement at the terminal is only 650, there will be a serious need for alternative employment opportunities.

91 Platform construction yards at Nigg, Ardersier and Kishorn have full order books, while Lewis Offshore at Arnish, Stornoway have secured sufficient contracts to maintain an employment level of around 500.

Scottish Council

92 We decided to join the Scottish Council (Development and Industry) following recent changes in the emphasis of their work. A form of agreement governing the board's relationship with the council in matters of common interest has been agreed by both parties. We contributed £1,000 towards the prize fund set up by the council for their 'Enterprise Scotland' business competition and participated in the panel which judged entries from the Highlands and Islands. We are also represented on the Highland area committee of the council.

Marketing

93 We continued to place emphasis on advisory and supporting services in the marketing field, which became even more important in view of the fairly general recession in retail trading conditions. Many firms in the craft and giftware industry suffered from a lack of forward orders, particularly noticeable in the sales of 'non essential' gift items which were hardest hit by a marked downturn in seasonal spending by tourists coming to the Highlands and Islands. Retail buyers attending trade shows restricted the value of orders placed to reduce their stock levels and this had the effect of raising stock holdings on the part of many of the producing firms. We encouraged local companies to increase their sales promotion activities, and were able to provide direct assistance in some cases. The knitwear industry was one of those to suffer most from the difficult trading conditions. The impact on individual firms varied considerably, with firms in the Western Isles generally hardest hit. Many retail gift shops closed down altogether, a symptom of the general malaise.

94 One of the most important trade shows in our marketing calendar is the International Spring Fair at the National Exhibition Centre, Birmingham. This year we took stands in three separate halls and sponsored participation by 19 different firms who shared the stands. In addition, three other firms from the Highlands and Islands had their own stands at the fair. Business reflected the general recession but the longer established and more sophisticated companies were not as badly affected as those who had entered the market more recently or had a less professional approach to selling.

95 We were involved in three major overseas trade shows during the first part of the year — the International Sports Equipment Fair (ISPO) held in Munich, the Salon International de l'Agriculture in Paris, and the Offshore

Technology Conference and Exhibition held in Houston. Two companies from Aviemore, manufacturers of carbon fibre skis and knitted sports headwear, participated in the Munich exhibition and were well pleased with the results of their first venture into the European winter sports market. In the Paris Agricultural Show, where we were associated with the Scottish Development Agency, we provided space in the food hall, principally with the object of promoting sales of Scotch beef and lamb, although we also promoted sales of Scottish beer, whisky, cakes and confectionery, as well as mounting a tourist information kiosk. At the Offshore Technology Exhibition in Houston, we assisted exhibits by a manufacturer of electronic equipment from Wick and Underwater Trials Ltd from Fort William.

96 Our tenth Highland Trade Fair held in the Aviemore Centre in October attracted 160 firms, of which 25 were exhibiting for the first time. About 1600 trade buyers attended the fair, representing almost 1,000 different firms and including 25 buyers from overseas. Bearing in mind the rather poor tourist season and the general economic situation, we were greatly encouraged by the attendance. Most exhibitors were well pleased with the level of orders placed.

97 Sixteen companies under the joint sponsorship of the board and the SDA exhibited their products on the Scottish stand at the Toronto Fall Gift Show held at the Canadian national exhibition showground in September. This was the second joint venture with the SDA's Small Business Division at this important trade show and half of the companies attending were from the Highlands and Islands. Most were pleased with the value of orders taken, allowing for the strong pound and trading conditions in Canada which were not dissimilar to conditions in our home market.

98 Earlier in the year, we were represented on a trade mission to the Faroe Islands organised by the development department of the Highland Regional Council. Twelve firms participated in the mission and achieved satisfactory results.

99 In May we shared a joint stand with Highland Craftpoint and the Small Business Division of the SDA at the new British Crafts Trade Fair held in Harrogate. The fair served a useful purpose in introducing the services of Highland Craftpoint to potential clients, although — not surprisingly in present circumstances — it could not be regarded as a commercial success in terms of orders taken by the crafts producers who rented space at the show.

100 During the year 50 new manufacturers had products accepted for registration within the board's 'Craftmade' labelling scheme. There are now 457 manufacturers registered to use the Craftmade label on their products. The label guarantees that items bearing it have been manufactured in the Highlands and Islands and is a safeguard for the manufacturer, the retailer and his customers.

101 The board's 'Shetland Mark' knitwear label continues to be widely used by knitwear producers in Shetland, but the absence of unanimous support restricts our ability to promote the mark as the sole guarantee of a genuine Shetland article. Shetland Islands Council continued to discuss with the local industry the possibility of achieving unanimous support for a mark controlled by the council, and we have indicated that we will collaborate with them in any measures designed to promote the long term survival and prosperity of the industry. Meanwhile over 157,000 swing tickets for use on Shetland garments were issued by the board during the year.

102 Our staff dealt with 254 trade enquiries or requests in 1980, many of which led to additional business for manufacturing and crafts firms in the area. In one instance, we were instrumental in negotiating an initial order worth £10,000 to the firm concerned. Our display centre in Inverness recorded over 11,000 enquiries about Highland products from the general public, many of which resulted in direct sales for retail outlets in Inverness and district.

Technical services

103 We have been increasingly involved in assisting companies with technical studies aimed at improving efficiency, and some encouraging results have been achieved. Requests for this service have to some extent been stimulated by added pressures on working capital resources, and also by the impact of our business workshops in making management personnel aware of the benefits of such studies. Four comprehensive studies were undertaken in the latter part of the year, and follow-up visits were made to help with the implementation of the new procedures and with redesign of equipment where necessary. Our staff were also involved in several other projects concerning specific problems such as factory layout, materials handling, and plant and machinery.

Temporary employment

104 We continued to support projects carried out under the Manpower Services Commission's special programmes scheme for providing temporary jobs for the unemployed. As in previous years, financial assistance was made available to sponsors of projects to help meet the materials and administration costs. The majority of these projects were sponsored by local authorities and included environmental schemes of benefit to local communities, the creation of new roads into peat banks, pier and jetty improvements and the provision and upgrading of village halls and sports facilities. We approved assistance for 51 projects located in various parts of the Highland Region and the Western Isles, providing an estimated 264 temporary jobs, 21 of which were for young people under the age of 19.

Training

105 We devoted a good deal of effort to the provision and encouragement of systematic training, both within individual firms and through various schemes designed to cater

for the needs of different industries or to help individuals in the acquisition of particular skills. Our expenditure in this field was largely matched by contributions from the European Social Fund. The fund approved our total claim in respect of estimated training expenditure for 1980. Although assistance from the fund is channelled partly to the Treasury in reimbursement of board expenditure on industry-wide or general training schemes, the benefit of the remainder is now felt directly by individual companies who implement their own in-house training schemes in consultation with the board. The board's contribution to the cost of such training schemes is now matched by a payment from the fund to the companies concerned.

106 Firms who received assistance for in-house training schemes spanned a number of different industries — for example, printing and computerised typesetting, knitwear manufacture, glassmaking, fish processing and pottery. Most of the firms concerned were located on the mainland, although we were also able to give some assistance in the Western Isles.

107 We maintained our 50% contribution towards the cost of the itinerant instructional service on maintenance of farm machinery and welding organised by the Agricultural Training Board. Under our ancillary employment training scheme a number of people in crofting and other communities received both advice and financial assistance towards courses of instruction for a variety of crafts and skills. These included pottery, weaving, sheepskin curing, machine knitting and upholstery.

108 A full report on a survey of employers' needs for training services in mid-Argyll and Kintyre, commissioned in 1979, was completed by the Scottish Council Research Institute for the board and the Training Services Division of the Manpower Services Commission. The report indicated that the three types of craftsmen for which an improvement in local training facilities is most needed are carpenters/joiners, electricians and vehicle mechanics. It also drew attention to the need to develop some institutional framework for bringing employers together to define training needs and develop ways of meeting these needs. We are following up the recommendations of the report in conjunction with the joint training group for the Highlands and Islands.

109 Our own staff carried out a survey of companies in the Highlands and Islands to assess their future needs for employees with a knowledge of electronics. The survey indicated that there would be an increasing demand for such employees, and preliminary discussions have taken place with Inverness Technical College on the implications for training facilities. The results of the survey have been

circulated to the participating companies, along with suggested syllabuses for three new courses in electronics as a basis for early discussion.

110 The joint training group compiled a correspondence course in book-keeping and basic accountancy designed in 13 weekly parts for the use of small businesses in the area. The object is to instruct the proprietor or his staff in the necessary practical skills required to produce information for management, government agencies and banks. Each unit includes lessons, examples, questions, model answers and comment, and builds into a useful work of reference. The group also introduced a self-learning book-keeping package for farmers, crofters and foresters. An initial programme of short specialised courses, completed in the summer, proved very successful. It was supported by employers from Shetland to Campbeltown, and offered training in basic management skills, finance for the non-accountant, stock control, recruitment and selection of staff, and many other topics. A second programme of short courses was drawn up to cover the period from September 1980 to May 1981.

111 We organised two short business workshops during the year, in Lerwick and Lochgilphead. The main topics covered were employment legislation, production layout, health and safety, recruitment and selection and leadership skills. The individual instructional and discussion sessions were led by a senior representative of the Advisory Conciliation and Arbitration Service and our own staff. The workshops were extremely well received by those attending, who were mainly proprietors or managers of small businesses.

Schools industry liaison

112 For the first time a pupil from the Highlands won the annual BP schools essay competition for the North of Scotland, sponsored by BP and organised jointly by the board (in Highland Region) and the Robert Gordon's Institute of Technology. The first prize for 1979 (announced early in 1980) was won by a pupil from Alness Academy, and three of the other five prizes went to pupils from schools in the Highland Region. The fifth BP schools lecture, intended for boys and girls aged 14/15 with a view to encouraging them to consider careers in engineering or technology, was held at Inverness Technical College in September.

113 Bearing in mind the ever-increasing relevance of an understanding of the technology and applications of electronic equipment to industrial and commercial activity, we are keen to encourage the development of education and training in this sphere at both secondary school and technical college levels. We were, therefore, extremely pleased to learn that the Highland Regional Council were purchasing micro-computers for installation in all of their senior secondary schools and technical colleges, and agreed to contribute £13,000 towards the cost of ancillary and peripheral equipment which would enable the schools and colleges to make the fullest possible use of the micro-

computers. We had two meetings with HM Inspectors of Schools to discuss how we could best contribute further to the development of electronics education throughout the Highlands and Islands, and discussion is continuing. Meanwhile, we have advised other education authorities about the assistance we have been able to give to the Highland Region, and indicated that we would be prepared to provide similar assistance elsewhere in the Highlands and Islands.

114 We contributed £1,000 towards the costs incurred by the Association of Agriculture in maintaining an office in Scotland, on the understanding that the association would devote part of their efforts to the Highlands and Islands. The association works to produce a better understanding of agriculture in schools, and implemented projects to encourage contacts between third and fourth year pupils of Secondary schools in Oban, Lochgilphead and Campbeltown and the agricultural community. The association has been studying the possibility of involving estate owners and farmers in 'in service' training courses for teachers in farming and countryside subjects. The purpose is to give teachers, many of whom have an urban background, guidance on how to organise class visits to the countryside and use them to best advantage.

115 The Organisation for Economic Co-operation and Development (OECD) are currently undertaking a project among member countries to examine the relationship between education and local development. We have contributed information to the rural study which focusses on non-formal and vocational education, and youth programmes within the Highland Region. OECD have also commissioned several case studies, one of which examines the parts played by the HIDB, Training Services Division, and the further education colleges in the provision and development of vocational education and training. The project will conclude with an international conference in Stornoway in 1981.

Transport

116 The board's specialist staff supply objective and expert advice on detailed transport problems, particularly in the freight transport field, for industrial and other transport users in the area. They also provide a source of information to help the board and other public bodies in taking decisions on many different questions relating to the provision of modern transport infrastructure and services within, or providing access to, the Highlands and Islands. Transport developments are still very much a subject of public interest, and our staff were active in contributing to community discussion and information in this field, as well as in various professional associations.

117 As part of our efforts to disseminate information and promote exchanges of views in the transport field, we organised a two-day freight transport seminar in Dunoon in

October, in conjunction with a materials handling and transport exhibition. The subjects covered ranged from road improvements to EEC legislation. Contributors included Sir Robert Lawrence, chairman of the newly formed National Freight Company and vice-chairman of the British Railways Board, and Mr Kenneth Munro, assistant to the director general for transport in the EEC.

118 In written evidence to the Armitage Committee on lorries, people and the environment, we supported the introduction of heavier goods vehicles because of the economic benefits to operators and the industries and traders they serve. Our views were vindicated by the committee's report, published by the Department of Transport in December.

119 Discussions were held with members of the British Road Federation about the conditions of Highland roads and improvements needed in the light of the EEC legislation reducing driving hours for buses and commercial vehicles. We submitted evidence to the Freight Transport Association on cases throughout the Highlands and Islands where road transport operators will face difficulty in conforming with the eight-hour limit on the driving day imposed by the EEC as from January 1981.

120 We were pleased that our representations on the fitting and calibration of tachographs on buses and commercial vehicles helped secure a temporary relaxation until the end of 1981 for island-based operators. The Department of Transport also agreed to set up special stations in remote areas.

121 November saw the opening of Orkney's first major road haulage warehouse and depot which we helped finance on Hatston Industrial Estate, Kirkwall. The company concerned have built up a daily road freight service between Kirkwall and Aberdeen, incorporating onward delivery of goods to and from destinations in Scotland, England, Ireland, Wales and the continent.

122 In December we invited all round-timber hauliers in Scotland to a meeting in Inverness with the purpose of forming an association to encourage bulk buying of tyres, spare parts, fuel, insurance, and possibly round-timber for selling to national and international outlets. The response was excellent and the Round Timber Transport & Trading Association was duly formed.

123 The Caledonian MacBrayne shipping services advisory committees continued to serve an extremely useful purpose as a means of discussing and clarifying matters of mutual concern to Calmac and their customers. We are represented on all three committees, serving Western Isles North, Western Isles South, and the Clyde area.

124 We have been involved in various efforts to make coastal bulk shipping operations more attractive and economical to shippers throughout the area. The development of roll-on, roll-off haulage traffic on subsidised ferry operations has made it more difficult for bulk cargo operators to compete, but we believe that the successors to the traditional 'puffers' have an important continuing role in the transport of commodities in the West Highlands and Western Isles. We have expressed this view in discussions with the Scottish Development Department, and by the end of the year were hopeful that the Government would provide a measure of financial assistance to ensure the continuation of these important services. With a view to extending the market for operators, trial shipments of round-timber and seaweed meal were arranged from Ardrishaig and Barcaldine to the Clyde area.

125 The year was a difficult one for air transport in the United Kingdom as a whole, with falling traffic and continuing increases in costs. Services in the Highlands and Islands fared slightly better than the norm. Some routes continued to show significant traffic growth and any reductions in passenger traffic were smaller than elsewhere.

126 Nevertheless, the financial pressures on air services in the board's area have been severe, particularly through airport user charges despite a welcome £2.7 million deficit subsidy from Scottish Office. The subsidy for Highlands and Islands airports cushioned the effect of the cost increases but only to a small extent, particularly for third level air service operators.

127 Two new scheduled air services were started during the year, a direct service between Edinburgh and Kirkwall by Loganair, and one between Glasgow and Wick via Aberdeen by Air Ecosse. Loganair withdrew the twice-daily scheduled service between Inverness and Edinburgh. The effects of improved road access between the two centres and rising airport charges were among the reasons given for termination of this service. Loganair also moved the base of operation for their Shetland inter-island services from Sumburgh Airport, run by the Civil Aviation Authority, to the airstrip at Tingwall, operated by Shetland Islands Council. The inter-island flights, in danger of being withdrawn in November 1980, were continued with the help of a subsidy from Shetland Islands Council to cover the period up to the end of March 1981.

128 In the light of encouraging traffic results during the first year of operation of the scheduled helicopter service between Glasgow and Fort William, we increased the level of our financial support. This enabled the operators to increase the frequency of the service to nine round trips per week, from May onwards, introducing a day return facility for business and other travellers. We also approved further support to

enable extension of the service to Oban, Lochgilphead and Rothesay. This development was unfortunately delayed, mainly by problems of planning approval in respect of the provision of helipads at the locations concerned. However, it appeared likely that these problems would be resolved early in 1981.

Tourism

129 1980 was a disappointing season. For the first time in many years the number of visitors to the Highlands and Islands decreased, by about 10% compared with 1979. This decline also occurred in many other holiday areas of the UK and in a number of established international tourist destinations. The causes were related to the international economic recession, inflation, unemployment and the strength of sterling against many other currencies.

130 It is encouraging to note, however, that the industry is responding positively to the recession and planning constructive action to overcome the problems and ensure that tourism in the Highlands and Islands will be even more secure in the future. We will take the necessary action to develop the assets of the Highlands and Islands for the future, and we are confident that our policies will complement and support steps being taken by the industry.

131 The development and improvement of the area's tourism facilities continued throughout 1980. The recreational assets of the Highlands and Islands will be an important factor in the future development of tourism and we hope to give a lead to the industry by formulating and implementing policies for the development of a variety of recreational facilities.

132 Co-operation in efforts to market the area's tourism product continued in 1980. In particular, hoteliers sought to maximise their promotional effectiveness by the formation of a number of marketing associations which we have been able to help. In the field of general promotion, efforts by the Highlands and Islands Tourism Council, the area tourist organisations, and the board were closely co-ordinated to achieve the largest promotional campaign yet mounted on behalf of the Highlands and Islands. The improvement and extension of future promotional activity is essential if the industry is to hold and increase its share of a fiercely competitive home and international market.

133 The year also marked a significant step forward with the introduction by the area tourist organisations, assisted by the board and the Scottish Tourist Board, of a voluntary

Local accommodation bookings

through tourist information centres from 1975 to 1980

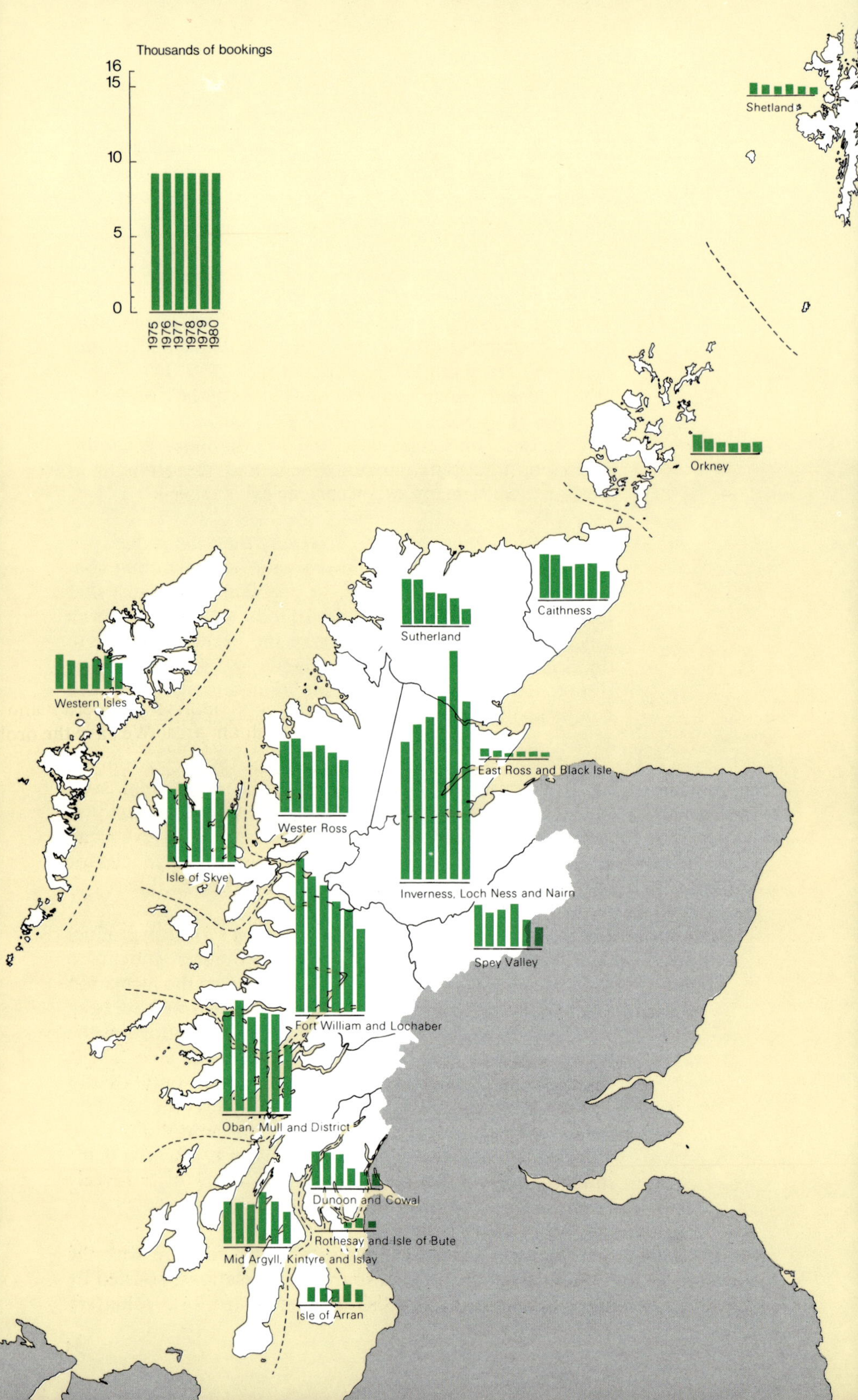

classification scheme for accommodation. The scheme should stimulate consumer confidence and lead to improvements in standards and service. We hope it will be the forerunner of a classification and grading scheme covering all accommodation facilities.

Facilities

134 The momentum built up in previous years in providing new tourism facilities, and expanding and improving existing services, continued throughout 1980, although there was some decline in the total number of enquiries for financial assistance. The overall trend remained constant, however, with most applications coming from small locally owned businesses in all parts of the area and involving relatively modest sums of money. The number of projects approved rose to 264, an increase of 15 over 1979, involving assistance of almost £4.4 million in the form of grants, loans and equity.

135 Many of the projects related to works being undertaken by the serviced accommodation sector, but in line with market demand in 1979 there was a significant increase in the number of self-catering applications. In all, 74 applications involving the development of 180 units were approved. At an average of just over two units per application, self-catering projects in the Highlands and Islands are low density, often providing supplementary income to some other form of economic activity. Assistance to self-catering also included the development of a number of touring caravan sites in key locations throughout the mainland.

136 The development of recreational facilities, in which the Highlands and Islands have considerable natural assets, will greatly assist in sustaining the future market for accommodation and catering businesses. We assisted 29 recreational projects in 1980 with marine related activities, particularly charter boats, constituting the greater part of investment. For the first time in a number of years, however, the expansion in charter fleet capacity was not matched by growth in market demand. Operators fared no worse than those in other parts of the UK, but further expansion may be delayed. The introduction of flotilla sailing did signify an attempt to open up new markets.

137 During the year work began on the conversion of Borrodale House, Raasay, into a 15 bedroom hotel which should open for business in the summer of 1981. At the end of the year negotiations were taking place with a private developer for the conversion of Borve Lodge in Harris into an hotel.

138 Stready progress was maintained on development proposals for reclaimed land at Ballachulish, a scheme jointly initiated by the Scottish Tourist Board, Scottish Development Agency, Highland Regional Council and the board. Work commenced on the information/interpretive centre, and by the end of the year initial submissions from developers

proposing major tourism facilities on the site were being assessed.

139 We reviewed our policy on winter sports development and also participated in a winter sports development working party chaired by the Highland Regional Council. After taking into account factors such as market demand, existing capacity, physical conditions, comparative development costs and conservation issues, we reaffirmed our support for major expansion of winter sports facilities on Cairngorm and minor developments elsewhere in the Spey Valley. The lack of clear evidence of demand raises doubts about the viability of major development at Ben Wyvis, while climatic and topographic conditions would make the slopes of Aonach Mor near Fort William a difficult development option. It may be, however, that more suitable slopes could be identified in the vicinity of Fort William.

140 Following this policy review we approved financial assistance for the creation of a day lodge on Cairngorm, which will provide a major shelter area, ticket offices, first-aid rooms, ski hire and catering facilities. Discussions held with the management of White Corries Limited could result in further development on the Glencoe ski slopes.

141 We adopted two further strategies during the year — for water sports development in Argyll and Bute, and for recreational development in the Great Glen. Both strategies seek to identify the different types of facilities required and to encourage public and private investment, in an effort to ensure full realisation of the significant economic potential inherent in the recreational assets of the areas. To secure the early implementation of the projects identified in both strategies we have agreed to appoint a water sports development officer for a three-year period.

142 Other projects being progressed by, or involving the board during the year, included a study of the potential for the development of a wet weather centre in Fort William and the rehabilitation of tenement property for self-catering accommodation in Rothesay.

Area tourist organisations

143 The servicing activities of area tourist organisations reflected the decline in the number of visitors. Accommodation booking figures, local and advance, dropped by 20%. Fewer visitors also affected the financing of the organisations, since an important element of ATO income is drawn from sales of goods and services. Nevertheless, the network made good progress in efforts to raise standards and improve the range of local promotional and informative literature.

144 The tourist information centre development programme continued with new centres being opened in Lerwick, Kirkwall, Helmsdale, Bettyhill, Lochinver and at Strathpeffer, where the information centre forms part of the visitor

complex at the old station buildings. Busy main centres in Portree and Fort William were improved. The long term programme to provide an adequate information centre network within the Highlands and Islands is now almost complete. The network is supplemented by a number of unmanned tourist information points providing local basic information and situated in lay-byes and other locations throughout the area.

145 The formation of a branch of the Cunninghame Tourist Association on the island of Cumbrae resolved negotiations to bring the island into the ATO network. The branch constitution is modelled on standard ATO lines and Cumbrae should now be able to participate in many of the ATO activities. The board also agreed to reconsider the possibility of amalgamating the two Ross-shire ATO's and to extend Skye ATO to include Lochalsh. Discussions on these proposals were underway at the end of the year.

146 The area tourist organisation is becoming an increasingly significant mechanism for development, and 1980 saw a major advance with the introduction of a voluntary classification scheme for accommodation establishments. Based on a three-category system introduced by the English Tourist Board, the scheme will be of considerable assistance to the holiday visitor and should also encourage accommodation units to upgrade their facilities.

147 Despite financial constraints the network managed to play a more effective role in the promotion of the Highlands and Islands through participation in exhibitions at Newcastle, Manchester and in London. Many of the organisations undertook additional advertising in an attempt to boost visitor numbers midway through the season.

Tourism Council

148 The general promotion of the Highlands and Islands as a holiday destination was again undertaken by the Highlands and Islands Tourism Council. As an outcome of detailed discussion on the results of marketing efforts in previous years, the council reallocated their budget in favour of increased advertising and promotional activity. To promote the 1980 season 125,000 copies of a full colour 28 page brochure were distrubuted by a variety of methods — press and TV advertising, exhibitions, and tourist boards.

149 The council made another important contribution to the development of the area by establishing their distribution headquarters in Golspie in premises provided by the board. Initially, the centre will provide seasonal employment for up to 14 people in East Sutherland and the council are considering ways in which permanent employment can be created.

150 During the year the council had constructive discussions with Sir Henry Marking, chairman of the British Tourist

The distribution centre established by the Highlands and Islands Tourism Council at Golspie, Sutherland.

Authority, and Mr Alan Devereux, chairman of the Scottish Tourist Board.

Marketing

151 The board's marketing efforts in 1980 were the most intensive to date. The major print item produced for the home market was the 36-page 'Holiday Ideas' brochure which featured 148 individual holidays of a widely differing nature. A total of 100,000 brochures were distributed in response to advertising campaigns in the press and on TV, from exhibition stands and through travel trade retail outlets, and early bookings were encouraging.

152 Our promotional work for winter sports is totally geared to the UK market. We continued an experiment with Ellerman Travel, who concentrated their efforts on the promotion and distribution of 100,000 brochures. During the period of operation of the holidays, from late November 1979 to the end of April 1980, the total income generated by the programme was just over £100,000. This package holiday co-operation was also carried through to the summer season with the joint production of a series of activity holiday packages featuring golf, sailing, fishing and riding as well as general touring.

153 The public transport rover ticket 'Travelpass' is used both in the UK and overseas and a total of 2,475 tickets were sold in 1980. This important marketing tool, used to boost visitor use of the area's public transport services, is now available through British Rail in seven overseas countries.

154 As a result of the area tourist organisations and the tourism council undertaking a greater share of marketing in the UK, the board have been able to devote more effort to overseas promotional work than in previous years. Wherever possible we conducted much of this work in co-operation with statutory agencies such as the BTA and with private enterprise.

155 In conjunction with the BTA and Northwest Orient Airlines, we organised a tourism trade mission to the USA in February which covered nine cities in 21 days. A total of 450 US travel agents and tour operators had the opportunity to learn of the tourism facilities operated by the 16 representatives from the Highlands and Islands who took part in the mission. Lord Mansfield, Minister of State with responsibility for tourism, joined part of the mission and we were pleased to show him one aspect of our overseas marketing activity. The mission coincided with the introduction of the 'Highland Fling' package holiday programme — a series of Highlands and Islands holidays designed exclusively for the United States market, promoted in conjuction with Northwest Orient Airlines and available through the US travel trade. We undertook further marketing work at BTA workshops in Canada and the USA and in the 'Sell Scotland' mission which visited Houston, St Louis and Atlanta.

156 Apart from our travel trade work, which involved staff in nine workshops at home and in Europe, the main public promotions undertaken on the continent were in holiday exhibitions through our co-operative effort with four Scottish regional authorities. Nine exhibitions were featured in the programme, including Paris, Frankfurt, Vienna, Utrecht and Brussels. A composite brochure covered the holiday attractions of the participating regions and, specifically for the Highlands and Islands, we distributed 66,000 Highland Holidaycard brochures, printed in appropriate language versions.

157 An additional advertising campaign was conducted in the middle of the 1980 holiday season in an effort to counteract disappointing early season results. The campaign complemented similar efforts by the Scottish Tourist Board and the individual area tourist organisations, and used television advertising in order to reach as wide an audience as quickly as possible.

158 To develop further markets for the Highlands and Islands we formulated a conference marketing policy during the year. The policy provides for the consideration of financial assistance for the development of conference related facilities, as well as a greater involvement in marketing.

Research

159 As in previous years we conducted hotel and self-catering occupancy studies and an analysis of the accommodation bookings made through the information centre network. These statistics are used in conjunction with statistical information from a number of other agencies to monitor progress and to compare performance with previous years.

160 During the year we received the intitial feasibility study on the development of tourist facilities based on the region's angling resources, and the final version of the Argyll and Bute water sports development study. In both cases we are pursuing a number of opportunities raised in these reports.

Argyll and Bute watersports study

Development proposals

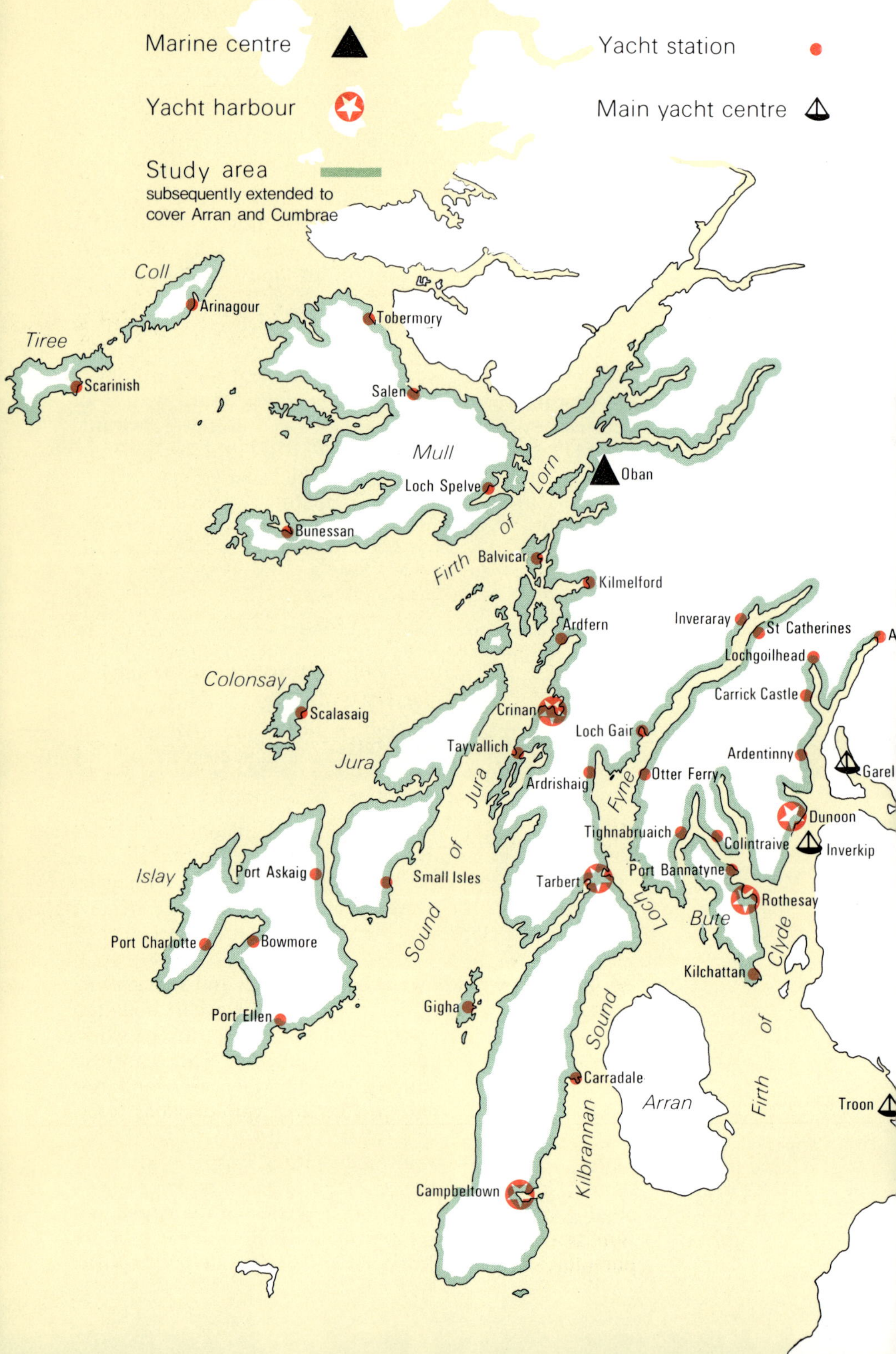

Additional research has been commissioned on water sports to provide similar information for Arran and the Cumbraes.

161 We made finance available to area tourist organisations to conduct local research studies and these have resulted in information being gained on visitors to Dunoon and Cowal, on hotel visitors in Orkney, and on usage patterns at a new major picnic site on the A9 trunk road.

162 The major element of the board's 1980 tourism research programme was a visitor expenditure survey. The basic field work took place during 1980 and the final report is due in 1981. It should yield valuable information on the detail of expenditure by holiday visitors to the Highlands and Islands which in turn can be used in planning the most effective future development.

163 We combined with the Scottish Tourist Board and other agencies to sponsor a major Scottish tourism and leisure patterns study. This will be the first major study of basic patterns of tourism recreation in Scotland since 1973 and should provide valuable up-to-date information.

164 The application of modern communications technology to the tourism industry presents a wide variety of opportunities to add to the competitive, efficient and cost effective aspects of the tourism industry in the Highlands and Islands. Recognising the significance of this technological application, the board commissioned a study to investigate the application of computerisation to the Highlands and Islands tourism industry. A wide ranging study, it will take into account public and private sector demands, the needs of the visitor and supporting administrative services, and must be applicable at both large and small scales of operation.

Liaison

165 Good liaison is essential if our objectives are to be achieved successfully. We are in constant contact with a variety of private sector interests and public agencies in the development and marketing of Highlands and Islands tourism, particularly with the BTA, STB and local authorities.

Fisheries

Landings

166 Fish landings in Scotland for 1980 totalled 371,312 tonnes valued at £114 million, an increase of 16,000 tonnes but a decrease of £8 million on the previous year. Of this 182,795 tonnes valued at £34 million were landed in the Highlands and Islands. As in 1979, a total ban on herring landings was maintained on the recommendation of fishery scientists, with the exception of a limited fishery in the Firth of Clyde and around the Isle of Man. Mackerel landings from the north west Scottish grounds were kept at approximately 100,000 tonnes but because of a fall in prices the value was reduced.

167 All sections of the catching side of the industry were adversely affected throughout the year. In addition to four further increases in the price of fuel, which led to heavier operating costs, interest charges on borrowed money rose steeply. These were accompanied by reduced prices at first hand sales, partly because of a large increase in imports. These impositions, together with smaller catches, presented fishermen with many problems, the most severely affected being those who had taken delivery of new high-cost vessels during 1979. The purchase price of second-hand boats dropped quite markedly during the year and a number of owners considering the purchase of new boats found that a substantial financial shortfall had to be bridged with expensive borrowed money.

168 For the major part of the year, the falling prices of fish was probably the most significant problem with which the catching side had to contend. This affected all species, but particularly the shellfish sector of lobsters and nephrops. Representations were made to the Government for some means of additional financial assistance until such time as agreement on the common fisheries policy had been concluded by the EEC. The Government responded by approving additional financial assistance of £17.1 million to the UK industry. A number of fishermen and their associations also approached the board for special financial assistance. In the main, however, we felt that we could help only by deferring, for a limited period, capital repayments on loans for boats in those cases where extenuating

circumstances prevailed. We felt that the Uists lobster fishermen came into this category. They had experienced a very poor 1979 season, when severe weather had curtailed their season to half its normal duration, and later faced depressed prices for lobsters because of imports.

169 During the mackerel season, larger vessels operate in fishing grounds traditionally used by creel boats. In the past a number of instances had demonstrated a total disregard of creel fishermen's gear. The position became so acute during 1980 that local men took their creels ashore until the end of the mackerel season. A solution to this pressing problem is urgently required.

Fishing plans

170 The Highland Regional Council and the Western Isles Islands Council drew up fishing plans during the year, in anticipation of a satisfactory conclusion to the common fisheries policy. It was generally expected that an agreed CFP would become a reality by the end of 1980 but, once again, agreement was delayed.

New boats

171 With the continued increase in the cost of new construction and the rapid escalation in operating costs, it is not surprising that interest in the purchase of both new and second-hand fishing boats remained low during 1980. We approved assistance for only one new 55ft boat during the year and six new shellfish/sea angling boats. We also assisted the purchase of 17 second-hand boats, a decrease of 12 on 1979.

Financial assistance

172 During the year we approved financial assistance of over £3.3 million for the fishing industry as a whole in the Highlands and Islands, an increase of £100,000 on 1979. The private contribution was just over £5.3 million, a substantial increase of £1.8 million. This reflects the increased contributions which fishermen now make towards the cost of their boats but, more significantly, several large fish farming projects with a substantial element of private sector finance were assisted in 1980. The total sum approved to all sectors of the industry since 1965 is now over £23 million at original cost. The breakdown of assistance for fisheries development as a whole in 1980 is shown below.

	HIDB		*Private*
	Grant	*Loan/ Equity*	*Sector Contribution*
Boats	£244,528	£1,438,642	£972,747
Fish processing, boatyards & ancillaries	168,200	317,130	423,800
Fish farming and freshwater fisheries	677,115	477,020	3,911,052
	£1,089,843	£2,232,792	£5,307,599

Processing

173 Fish processors had greatly improved supplies during the year although landings included a substantial increase in the percentage of small fish. Markets for small processed fish were severely depressed and competition was keen. On the

other hand quality inshore fish continued to meet good demand, pointing to a satisfactory future for small processors provided supplies continue to be available in sufficient quantities.

174 Supplies of fish for the drying factory at Breasclete improved considerably during the year although a proportion of the fish was purchased at high rates from Norwegian fishing vessels. The high prices the Norwegians require reflect the subsidised prices paid to fishermen in Norway. Catches from the remaining local long line boat were generally satisfactory with a larger proportion of ling and tusk being caught. Supplies were obtained from UK trawlers and from Faroes during the year and arrangements are being made for increased supplies from these sources in 1981.

Fish landings to the drying factory at Breasclete, Isle of Lewis, increased during the year.

175 One fish processing and hand filleting unit was established during the early part of the year and is operating with satisfactory supplies. A training programme for fish filleting is expected to begin early in 1981 to assist this and other similar units in the future. Plans for a further two small fish-processing units are well advanced although the companies involved have experienced delays in land acquisition.

176 Shellfish processing companies suffered considerable problems and some ceased trading. The difficulties were caused by two main factors: firstly, catches of prawns continued much longer than in past years and, secondly, the Spanish market stopped buying for a period. When trading with Spain recommenced, prices offered were at a much lower level. Towards the end of the year the markets for processed prawns started to firm up and it is hoped that this trend will continue.

177 The lobster market was very poor throughout the year as a result of cheap exports from Canada. In consequence, we approved a small project to encourage diversification of fishing effort from lobster to crab fishing in the Uists. This

will commence early in 1981 and, with the help of Torry Research Station, give fishermen in the Uists the opportunity to learn the appropriate processing methods.

178 We helped an Inverness-based venture to develop further and market shellfish products packed in brine. This project, which commenced in November, is showing good signs of progress with markets being obtained in both the UK and the continent. In Shetland, we gave financial assistance to the development and marketing of pet food produced from fish offal. The project is already showing signs of success in producing an acceptable product, and a marketing trial will commence early in 1981. The development is very important for the Shetland fish processing industry as it will greatly improve the value of fish offal. Experiments will be undertaken during 1981 to develop a product for human consumption, using the best quality processed fish offal.

Boatbuilding

179 The depressed economic condition of the fishing industry continued to affect adversely the boatbuilding effort in the UK and the Highlands and Islands. Few orders for new boats were placed as a result of the uncertainty about the future size of the fishing fleet and its composition, the amount of annual quotas from which to obtain viable returns, and the problems of repaying the large loans now required to fund a new boat.

180 Campbeltown Shipyard Ltd have again demonstrated the high quality of their boats by being able to obtain a sufficient workload to retain their labour force at 1979 levels. The yard have developed a new round-bilge design for what can be called a multi-purpose economy boat. With this type of vessel added to their range the firm should be in a position to take full advantage of any improvement in the market when agreement is finally reached on a common fisheries policy.

181 Robertsons of Sandbank Ltd, the last of the high quality moulders of GRP sailing craft, fast commercial vessels and motor cruisers in Scotland, went into liquidation with the loss of 90 jobs in the Dunoon area. The neighbouring boatyard, Morris and Lorimer Ltd, purchased the seaward portion of the yard and some workers were re-employed in handling vessels hauled out for winter storage. The moulds for the 35ft cruiser 'Highland Admiral', leased by the company just prior to closure, reverted to the board and we are exploring means of placing them to the best advantage.

182 A more effective slipway is planned by a boatyard on the Clyde to enable it to handle vessels up to 80ft in length and with greater breadth than was possible previously. The slip at Wick is being improved to enable vessels to be side-slipped and when fully operational should bring considerable advantages to the local boatyard. At Kyle of Lochalsh the small boatbuilding and engineering company, Messrs MacLean and Macrae, completed the fitting out of their largest vessel, a 54ft GRP fishing boat, and improved their

slipway to enable them to haul out Admiralty tenders and the largest inshore fishing vessels. The slip and jetty financed by the board at Portnahaven on Islay have been completed. It is hoped that an engineering company interested in using the facilities will be able to commence operations soon.

Fish farming

183 The pace of development in fish farming rose noticeably during 1980, with salmon farming continuing to lead the trout and shellfish sectors. Significantly, overall financial assistance by the board to commercial development during the year totalled £1.1 million, more than trebling assistance in 1979 and involving 11 new projects and the expansion of 7 existing businesses. Private investment in these developments, at almost £4 million, reflected the very considerable scale on which salmon farming in particular is now being attempted. We anticipate that 40 full-time jobs and 33 of a seasonal or part-time nature will be created when these projects are fully underway. Though the cost per job ratio in fish farming is high, it has to be recognised that they are totally new forms of development and in many instances are located in isolated areas where little opportunity for alternative development exists. The increase in our expenditure on research in 1980 highlighted the embryonic nature of the fish farming industry. Some 14 different research projects, a number of which are of an on-going nature, received assistance of £308,000.

184 Board assistance to fish farming now totals £5.8 million at original cost. Of this £4.2 million has been approved for commercial projects and £1.6 million for research and development. Private investment is now over £9 million. A total of 56 fish farming businesses have been assisted so far, 39 in salmonid production, 15 in shellfish, one eel farm, and one company involved in contract research work. Around 250 full-time and almost 120 part-time jobs have been created. To date, we have helped finance 57 research and development projects across a wide range of subjects.

185 Salmon farming continued to expand through increased production from existing units and new farms coming into operation. Long-term confidence appears unaffected by the various set-backs that inevitably occur through natural disaster, disease or predation. Although individuals in the area have set up a number of small enterprises, salmon farming continues to be the province primarily of the larger company with substantial financial resources to call on. This is hardly surprising bearing in mind the very considerable capital costs of establishing such units, the high risk nature of the venture and the long wait until profitability is achieved. For these reasons salmon farming cannot be readily regarded as one in which to encourage widespread local participation. We are hopeful, however, that on-growing by local people can be encouraged under the wing of established companies with the necessary expertise over the whole spectrum of activity. There is growing recognition

Fish farming activities

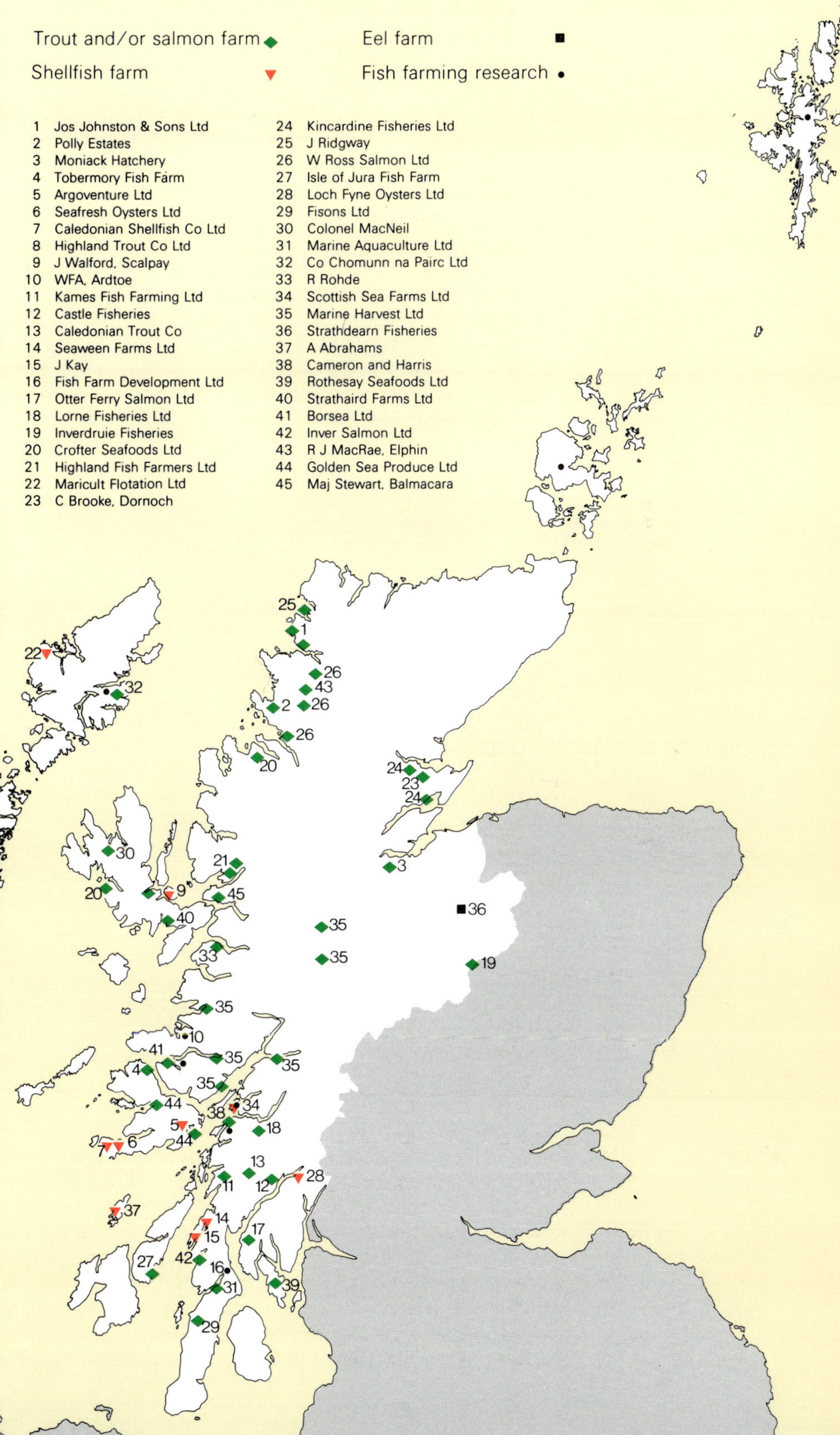

of the importance of marketing in salmon farming, and signs of greater co-operation between farmers to deal with increasing competition from Norwegian salmon farms and imported Pacific salmon. Smolt supply continues to be somewhat unpredictable in quality and quantity but as experience grows and research and development contributes to new technology, there is optimism that a more reliable pattern of supply will emerge. The more widespread occurrence of viral disease is causing considerable uneasiness, emphasising the now paramount need for more effective disease legislation.

186 In both 1979 and 1980, phytoplankton blooms occurred in two sea lochs and caused significant fish kills. Though the occurence of such toxic blooms had been recorded elsewhere, it was the first time fish kills were directly attributed to such outbreaks in Scottish west coast waters. As these blooms can affect shellfish as well as finned fish, the outbreaks have identified the need for research. In conjunction with other bodies, we hope to set in train research and development programmes that will provide much more data.

187 There has been no noteworthy increase in the development of trout farming in the board's area though a number of established units experienced in rainbow trout production have initiated expansion plans. During the year we approved financial assistance to Co-Chomunn na Pairc Ltd for the establishment of a 20 ton per annum trout on-growing unit in the Isle of Lewis, utilising floating pens in freshwater lochs. Commercial development in this case has followed a two-year trial designed to establish operational and financial parameters. Results were sufficiently encouraging to justify the step to commercial scale production. The trial was also designed to enable the formulation of a small-scale trout farming model that could be replicated in other suitable locations. As a result further trout on-growing units along similar lines may be established in Lewis over the next year, but one highly critical aspect is the necessity to establish additional markets for the product. The economics of small-scale trout units are such that premium prices must be obtained for the product, either by selling to local outlets or developing a higher priced, added value product to sell in a limited but exclusive market. The transition from supplying local outlets to developing a premium product for a luxury market will require careful preparation.

Shellfish

188 Growth in shellfish cultivation continued slowly through 1980, although general interest remained healthy with the promise of several new ventures being promoted in 1981. We assisted three projects in 1980, one on-growing oysters from purchased seed, the other two expanding existing mussel farming operations A greater proportion of effort in the shellfish sector was devoted to research and development in order to establish a suitable base for commercial growing. We have always held the view that shellfish cultivation could

be a more appropriate form of development for local encouragement than finned fish. The risk factor is less and no feed costs are involved, the shellfish feeding themselves from natural plankton supplies. With salmonid feed costs between £300 and £450 per ton, the significance of such an advantage becomes readily apparent. At the same time it has to be recognised that, as with all forms of fish farming, we have much to learn in terms of tried and tested technologies and it will be some time yet before the results of sustained research and development bear fruit in any significant expansion.

189 We supported shellfish research in suspended culture of scallops (including a pilot commercial project), bottom culture and reseeding of scallops, suspended culture of oysters and the development of hatchery techniques for scallop and abalone. Increased research effort will be directed towards mussel cultivation in the near future. The shellfish site testing programme, run over the past three years at some 25 locations in different west coast and island lochs, was concluded at the end of 1980. The task of collating the data and interpreting the results will be completed early in 1981. On behalf of the board, the White Fish Authority are continuing to eveluate a suspended culture system of oyster on-growing, based on a new reattachment technology.

190 The year saw increased interest by local parties in shellfish cultivation, particularly the islands councils of Shetland, Orkney and the Western Isles, all of whom are active in research and development which it is hoped will lead to commercial development. Shetland Islands Council have embarked upon an ambitious scheme of mussel cultivation with local on-growers, having first undertaken a comprehensive site-testing programme. In the early 70's, as part of the board's mussel raft trial scheme, a number of test rafts were made available for Shetland waters and it is encouraging to note that this initiative has been maintained to the point of commercial production. In conjunction with the Western Isles Islands Council, we plan commercial on-growing of mussels on a pilot scale basis in the coming year, involving interested local people. As in the case of Shetland, the local response has been encouraging.

191 The demand for cultivated shellfish from the board's area continues to be good, with the high quality products selling well, albeit to a currently limited market. The processing of mussels and oysters is under trial by some producers and the prospects for future co-operation in promotions and sales appear good.

Research

192 Our assistance towards fish farming research has, in the main, been directed towards development rather than pure research, taking care to avoid duplication with other research organisations. Our ability to assist research and development in fish farming is of considerable value, especially as so many areas require detailed study and

economic stringency has diminished the ability of other organisations to fund research.

193 Work by the White Fish Authority into the development of techniques for the commercial rearing of marine fish advanced considerably in 1980. Board assistance for the programme was primarily used to increase production of marine flat fish juveniles and for research facilities for both halibut and shellfish. For the first time good survivals were achieved throughout the rearing cycle and production of juvenile turbot exceeded targets. These juveniles will be available in 1981 for on-growing in water of ambient temperature and further trials to demonstrate the viability of turbot farming under commercial conditions.

194 Some preliminary investigations were made into halibut rearing techniques and funds were approved for a research programme to be carried out jointly by the White Fish Authority at Ardtoe and the Scottish Marine Biological Association at Oban. Some basic research was carried out on fertile halibut eggs obtained from Norway. In addition, a stock of juvenile halibut was collected from two commercial fishing vessels who co-operated in catching live fish to establish the basis of a future breeding population.

Training

195 In conjunction with Inverness Technical College, and with funding from the Training Services Division of the Manpower Services Commission and the European Social Fund, we continued the one-year fish farm training course designed primarily for husbandrymen. Twelve of the total intake of thirteen trainees who completed the course in 1980, all of whom belonged to the Highlands and Islands, found jobs in the fish farming industry. The Marine Harvest Ltd trophy for the outstanding student of the year went to Miss Vivienne Rollo, the first time it has been won by a female student.

196 The 1980/81 course commenced in August with a further fourteen students, almost all of whom were selected from the board's area. A total of 39 young husbandrymen and women have now completed the course, widening the pool of trained personnel. The course enjoys the co-operation and support of the industry which takes students for on-farm periods of practical training. Three blocks of four weeks each are spent at the technical college where students undergo intensive instruction in practical subjects such as building, welding, plumbing and hydraulics, electronics and engineering, and receive a grounding in academic subjects with emphasis on biology, chemistry, fish physiology and related studies. Short periods are also spent at Stirling University (on fish disease), the Scottish Marine Biological Association (marine studies, survey and hydrography) and at the White Fish Authority (marine fish cultivation).

197 A three-week course for non-graduates holding husbandry positions on fish farms was introduced in 1978. The course,

Sir Kenneth Alexander (front, third left) with successful students from the 1980 fish farming training course.

held annually at Inverness Technical College, was well supported in 1979 and 1980. It enables participants to up-date their knowledge of such varied subjects as fish physiology, nutrition and disease, legislation, engineering, net mending and emergency first-aid. We are actively pursuing with the technical college proposals for a permanent fish farm training facility on the west coast. Some progress has been made in identifying suitable facilities and sites.

Hatchery

198 The successful build-up of rainbow trout brood stock at our Moniack hatchery continued in 1980. This will increase the output of ova, fry and fingerlings, and we anticipate the production of some eight million ova in the winter of 1980/81. Imports of cheap ova into the UK caused some difficulties in sales, but the prospects for selling all of the winter's production both within and ourside the UK appeared good. The unfortunate spread of viral diseases places an even greater emphasis on the need to purchase stock from certified desease-free sources. DAFS Marine Laboratory continue to monitor the broodstock at the unit and provide the necessary certification.

Conference

199 The annual fish farming conference organised by the board and the Scottish Marine Biological Association was held at Oban in February. Attendance rose to a record 250 delegates representing Scottish, UK and foreign fish farming interests. The conference is firmly established and attracts fish farmers, research workers, consultants and others with interests in the development of the industry. The 1980 conference also included an exhibition of fish farming equipment by manufacturers.

Freshwater fisheries

200 Because of pressure of other work, we were unable to devote as much effort as we would have wished to the improvement of freshwater fisheries. Only one case was approved for financial assistance, and much of the research work in which we had participated previously had to be curtailed. We approved assistance for the Atlantic Salmon Trust to help finance an investigation into the impact of the Greenland Atlantic salmon fishery. A comprehensive report is available from the trust, which is to be commended for the work it does in the interests of the Atlantic salmon and its conservation.

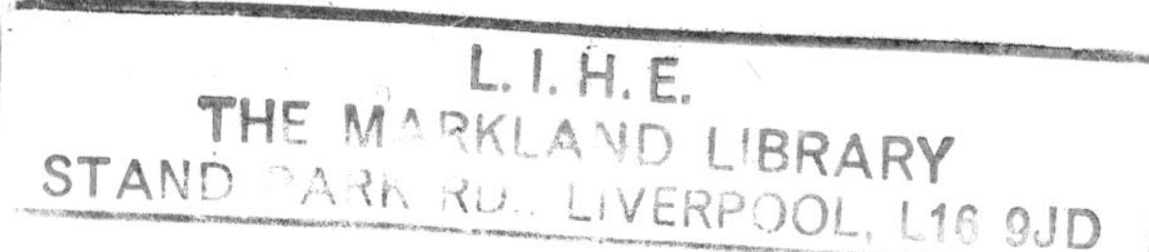

Land development

Trends

201 1980 will be remembered as a year of crucial significance to future land use trends in the Highlands and Islands. A range of adverse factors combined to burden the livestock sector with unprecedented problems, already proving insurmountable for some and undoubtedly leading to the demise of more agricultural businesses in the foreseeable future. These features were mainly the effects of a disastrous harvest in 1979, yet another poor season during 1980, and stagnant store cattle and hill lamb prices in the autumn resulting in seasonally high overdraft levels remaining unabated and, indeed, further increased by high interest charges.

202 The year will be remembered also for the closure of the Corpach pulp mill, which robbed the growing forest industry of an important market. Exports to Scandinavia provided a temporary solution to the sudden loss of the

Store livestock prices (actual)

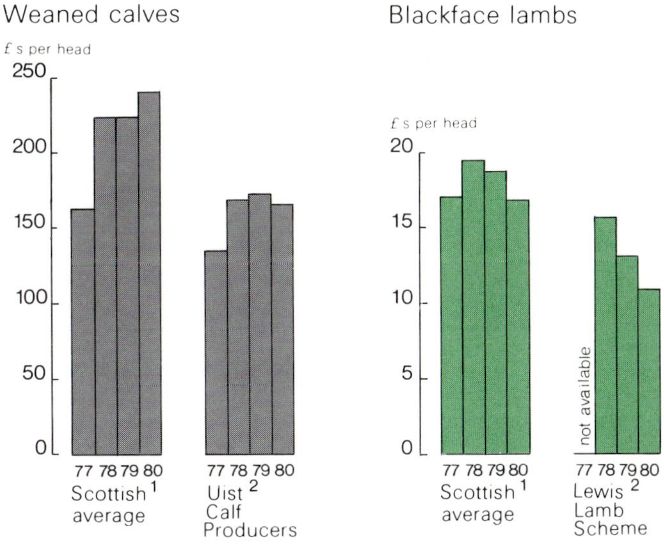

1 Unweighted averages of weekly sales returns as reported in "Scottish Farmer"
2 Derived averages from marketing schemes

market for small roundwood, and helped to soften the immediate impact of the closure on the forestry sector. The long awaited Government statement on forest policy, released in December, was reassuring in its positive attitude to the continuing role of forestry but in detail gave grounds for disquiet on behalf of Highland forestry.

203 Despite the background of adverse events in the rural land use sectors, the board's associated work continued to expand. Financial assistance to agricultural developments increased and we were particularly active, along with others, in drawing the attention of Government to the serious problems of the agricultural and forestry sectors. Progress continued with special schemes for livestock improvement and marketing, both for store livestock production in the remoter areas and for the finished stock, or deadmeat, at the other end of the production cycle. Deer management and farming were supported in a variety of ways, good progress was made on development of our peat resources, and emphasis continued to be placed on co-operation, syndication and less formal groupings as particularly appropriate vehicles for production and marketing development.

Policy

204 Early in the year it became increasingly apparent that if hill farmers and crofters were to recover from the financial setbacks of the previous two years, market returns or Government support would have to improve markedly in 1980. However, uncharacteristically depressed prices for hoggets and early lambs in the late spring and early summer of 1980, due mainly to a closed French market and a large increase in early lamb production on low ground in England, suggested that no such relief would stem from the market. In June, therefore, we made strong representations to the Minister of State on behalf of our sheep producers seeking ratification of a sheepmeat regime offering assured market prices in time for the main summer and autumn sales. The regime did not emerge until October and its effects were too late for store lamb producers.

205 We monitored livestock market prices in our area throughout the year and, relating these to regional input costs and other overheads such as interest charges, foresaw major problems for hill producers generally. We combined with the National Farmers' Union of Scotland and other agencies to argue vigorously to Government that special aid measures were needed urgently if the hill farming sector was to be protected from major damage through enforced disposal of its nucleus breeding stocks. We proposed a graded system of hill livestock compensatory allowances for hill cattle and sheep breeders or, at the very least, a significant increase in the prevailing flat rate payments. In the event, a 75p or 14% increase for sheep and a £7.50 or 21% increase for hill cattle headage payments were announced in November. Further, the EEC suckler cow premium scheme, offering £12.37 per beef breeding cow, had been announced from Brussels in October.

206 All of these additional payments are to be welcomed but it remains to be seen if these alone can help significantly to sustain the hill livestock sector through a hopefully kinder winter until the marketing season of 1981, which itself must show improvement if the industry is to survive. A major factor for the future recovery of the industry must be a further reduction in interest rates. Meantime, within our limited resources, we have tried to help the hardest hit cases which have run into difficulties in the middle of planned development programmes.

207 During 1979 we provided further information requested by the Scottish Office in relation to our proposals for more effective rural land use, originally submitted in 1978. Early in 1980 we were advised that the Secretary of State for Scotland did not intend to introduce measures to give effect to our proposals as they stood, but that the continuing exchange on the under-use of land — which, in our view, remains an area of major concern — had not been closed.

Financial assistance

208 During the year the assistance shown below was offered to agricultural, horticultural, contracting and related projects.

	Cases	*Loans*	*Grants*
		£	£
Shetland	15	13,550	15,930
Orkney	61	363,120	182,467
Caithness	18	90,430	46,583
North West Sutherland	2	3,000	350
South East Sutherland	3	29,000	7,400
West Ross	3	2,390	2,395
East Ross	14	46,850	72,740
Lewis/Harris	8	5,616	12,749
Uists/Barra	11	5,185	23,070
Skye	7	12,200	11,491
Inverness	21	149,000	129,945
Argyll	43	248,000	197,831
Nairn	8	13,750	240,615
Arran	7	39,200	14,618
Bute	7	88,000	61,750
Total	228	1,109,291	1,019,934

209 The number of cases offered assistance, at 228, represented a 21% increase on 1979, while financial assistance offered rose by 40%. The greatest proportion of aid, at 56%, was offered to 108 hill and upland farms and crofts.

210 As in recent years, Orkney and Argyll were the main recipients of assistance. The number of island cases assisted rose by 33 to 138 and represented 48% of total assistance. The following table summarises the increasing trend in aid to island areas.

	1976		1978		1980	
	No of cases	*Gross assistance* £000	*No of cases*	*Gross assistance* £000	*No of cases*	*Gross assistance* £000
Orkney & Shetland	13	95.1	47	396.0	76	575.1
Western Isles & Skye (a)	5	8.5	18	33.2	28	80.7
Argyll Islands (b)	15	91.4	14	118.4	34	324.1
Total	33	195.0	79	547.6	138	979.9

Notes: (a) Including Small Isles
(b) Including Arran & Bute

211 Towards the end of the year we completed an evaluation of the impact of the board's aid to agriculture. The main features of the findings were reassuring. Apart from a continuing increase in the take-up of board finance, largely in keeping with the occurrence of the main farming systems, the average physical and economic performance of farms helped by the board was substantially better than that for the average of all farms, over the six year period from 1974 to 1979 examined in the survey. Board assistance, offered mostly as loan finance to farms and crofts undertaking approved development schemes, averaged 30% of total project cost, with other statutory schemes providing an additional 10%. Total investment on the part of 919 board assisted projects had involved by the end of 1979 an estimated £25.3 million at 1978 prices. Interestingly, 70% of the applicants were below 45 years of age compared with only 24% of farmers in Highland Region being below that age. The most outstanding trends were increases of 48% and 13% in assisted farms' beef cow and hill ewe numbers compared with no change and a decline of 10% in the respective regional statistics. Full-time labour on the average assisted farm fell by 6% over the same period compared with 20% on the 'regional' farm.

212 Statistics of financial performance were similarly encouraging in the comparison, but it would be wrong to draw too many conclusions from the results. It is acknowledged that, even without board assistance, the same sample of units would probably show a considerably better than average performance. However, we find it reassuring that board finance appears in the main to be channelled into a progressive sector of the industry.

Livestock improvement

213 The board's livestock improvement working party continued to meet regularly. Recognising the pressures facing Shetland agriculture, the working party recommended that the agricultural advisory service be strengthened. As a result of this initiative, we have joined with Shetland Islands Council and the North of Scotland College of Agriculture to fund an additional adviser. The appointment, made in October, is for five years and is intended to improve the scope for tackling major problems such as common grazings, or 'scattald', and livestock improvement, as well as strengthening the general advisory effort.

214 Our heifer production scheme, devised by the working party for the Uists, Barra, Mull and Iona, is progressing satisfactorily and over 700 heifers have now been produced. The Department of Agriculture have carried out a number of heifer calf inspections and are satisfied with the quality of stock.

215 The working party is considering the scope for further work in the Western Isles and, in particular, a heifer rearing scheme for Lewis and Harris, and the Lewis artificial insemination service. Other possible developments in livestock marketing in the more difficult areas are being studied. Glenelg and some sheep stock clubs on Skye are examples of areas with possibilities for small-scale producer group marketing schemes.

Marketing

216 The year was a difficult one for livestock producers and the problems of livestock marketing generally, and store lambs in particular, were all too apparent. The board and the Central Council for Agricultural and Horticultural Co-operation have jointly funded a four-year research and development programme on livestock marketing. A marketing officer was appointed in late 1979 and, during 1980, he studied a wide range of marketing problems, working closely with existing organisations. The research phase of the programme will be completed in May 1981, to be followed by implementation of development proposals emerging from the research.

217 Lewis Livestock Ltd, a new co-operative which markets lamb and weaned calves, was formed early in the year and took over from the Lewis lamb marketing scheme formulated by the working party and run by the board during 1978 and 1979. The co-operative has over 200 members and marketed 2,000 store lambs and 25 weaned calves through auction marts in Inverness and Dingwall. Despite a difficult trading year, the co-operative performed well and the prospects for the future look bright.

218 The longer established Uist Calf Producers Ltd have traditionally sold weaned calves direct to feeding farmers, but in November 1979 they sold a small number of calves through a mainland auction mart. In 1980 they expanded this method of selling and sold over 150 weaned calves through auction rings in Perth, Dingwall and Inverness in October and November. Encouraged and assisted by the board to develop use of the auction system, they will continue to look closely at this method of selling for the future with a view to increasing their output and diversifying marketing options.

219 In Shetland, Northmavine Livestock Producers Ltd, a recently formed co-operative group of crofters and farmers, continued to operate their direct sale scheme to feeding farmers in Kincardineshire, selling nearly 1,000 Suffolk cross store lambs during 1980.

Highland meat

220 We continue to encourage the provision of adequate, modernised abattoir facilities in the area and several significant developments took place in 1980.

221 A prefabricated slaughterhouse unit was fully commissioned and operational on the Island of Mull in November, and local farmers and crofters have formed a co-operative, Mull Slaughterhouse Ltd, to manage the unit. The capital cost was met from a significant local contribution, together with grants from the board and Argyll and Bute District Council. A local man was appointed and trained as a part-time slaughterman. Demand for the service, although it will be highly seasonal, has been brisk from the outset, with throughput of several hundred sheep and a few cattle by the end of the year. Interest in this type of slaughterhouse has been expressed by small scale butchers in other remote areas.

222 Thurso slaughterhouse was extensively rebuilt and re-equipped, with board help, to comply with the new hygiene standards. It reopened in December and initial throughput was significantly higher than at the start of the year. The board have also co-operated in efforts to retain the services of Dingwall slaughterhouse, under threat of closure for much of the year. By the end of the year there were indications that a new tenant would undertake to operate the facility.

223 Orkney Islands Council's proposed meat complex took a major step when the knackery section was completed in early September. Work has commenced on the abattoir building which should be completed by the late summer of 1981. We continued to work with other interested parties on matters concerning the funding of the building and the formation of a company to operate the new meat complex. This company, Orkney Meat Ltd, will be formally registered early in 1981.

Forestry

224 The year was one of mixed fortunes for forestry, with much gloom amongst wood using industries but with afforestation reaching 12,000 hectares for the first time in several years.

225 We continued to press for a sustained afforestation level of the order of 13,000 hectares per annum in the Highlands and Islands, believing that this level will have to be sustained for another 20 years to allow the rational development of wood using industries. There is an urgent need for a broadening of the range of incentives for afforestation so as to be more attractive to all categories of landowners and tenants. We argued also for a planned development of wood using industry and for more detailed information on predicted wood availability for industry.

226 A statement of Government forestry policy was published in December and we were preparing to comment in some detail in early 1981. The Government proposed to reduce the exchequer contribution to forestry by the sale of Forestry

Commission assets. It remains to be seen exactly what is implied by this change. The policy statement was reassuringly positive in that the Government re-stated their belief in the value of forestry in the economy, which should have a significant effect in maintaining the confidence of private investors. However, no proposals were announced to tackle the difficult problems of the release of sufficient quantities of land to sustain planting rates. Normally, the Forestry Commission have roughly 75% of new forests in the board's area, but following lower levels of land acquisition the afforestation rate of the commission nationally is declining steadily. The Highlands and Islands may well be shielded from these reductions in the short term as the area contains half of all reserves of planting land, but in the medium term the effects are bound to be felt. If the Government's planting targets are to be met, private afforestation will have to expand to the same level as achieved by the Forestry Commission throughout the last decade. It is by no means certain that private investors will be as keen to plant substantial areas of poor ground.

227 Much work was undertaken during the year relating to the problem of wood using industries in a year of seriously depressed trading, especially with respect to the closure of the Corpach pulp mill in November. The prospects for any sort of major wood using plant to replace the pulp mill in the next few years appear poor, given the present chronic condition of the pulp and paper industry throughout the UK. We had anticipated an immediate and serious impact on forestry and timber haulage but this was largely averted by the export of small round-wood to Scandinavia. This market can only be regarded as a temporary one for the bulk of Highland forests, which are situated far from the east coast ports of exports. Efforts will be continued to find a more satisfactory solution.

228 The sawmilling industry also experienced a crisis. The year started with good production and full order books but the combined effects of the strength of sterling, high interest rates and world-wide recession in manufacturing and house building saw orders drop to a seriously low level by the end of the year. Prospects do not look good for at least the first six months of 1981 and those mills recently modernised with loan capital are in many instances in serious financial difficulty.

229 Despite this we were glad to assist a number of forestry contracting and sawmilling companies who were developing their activities, but enquiries were fewer than in recent years. We were particularly pleased to see the redevelopment of the Kilmallie Sawmill by Riddochs of Rothiemay Ltd, which we assisted jointly with other Government departments. The mill will be one of Europe's largest and make comprehensive use of micro-electronics. Our total contribution to forestry contracting and sawmilling, excluding the Kilmallie mill,

consisted of £66,000 grant, £173,000 in loans and £23,000 in interest relief grant.

Peat

230 Continuing our attempts to develop the peat resources of the Highlands and Islands, we undertook small projects to supply sample quantities of particular peats for both industrial and horticultural use and for the testing of markets and techniques for small scale production. We helped a number of companies to research possible developments, frequently with very close co-operation from the peat section of the Macaulay Institute for Soil Research. A study of the horticultural market in Holland, in association with a Dutch company, concluded that Caithness peat was not yet a viable source of supply in the short term, but the position will be kept under review. An area of recent increased interest has been the greater use of peat for energy, including electricity generation. It is too early to draw conclusions about large scale uses of peat for energy, although there appears to be a good case for the expansion of the commercial supply of domestic fuel peat on a local basis. Our exhibit on peat at the Royal Highland Show in June generated a great deal of interest among visitors.

Mechanised peat cutting near John o' Groats, Caithness.

Horticulture

231 After a fairly good early spring, weather conditions deteriorated as the year progressed with increasingly wet and overcast conditions from mid-summer onwards. Although horticultural production was not too badly affected, seed germination and weed control were poorer than normal in some areas. Fruit, vegetable and hardy nursery stock growers had a fairly successful year, but for many the constantly rising costs of production and high interest rates reduced profit margins significantly.

232 Enquiries for financial assistance for horticultural developments of all kinds remained high throughout the year. Fifteen projects were assisted to the extent of £78,635, including new units and the expansion of existing ones in market gardening, fruit, tomato, herb and hardy nursery stock production.

233 In addition to these commercial projects, we participated financially in other more innovative aspects of production and marketing. Jointly with the Central Council for Agricultural and Horticultural Co-operation, we are meeting the cost of a systematic promotional campaign within the Highlands for locally grown market garden crops. These are marketed as 'Highland Grown' by a group of seven farmers in the Ross-shire, Inverness-shire and Nairn areas who embarked on an 80-acre cropping programme in 1980. An experienced full-time field officer was appointed to co-ordinate production, grading and packaging and a wide range of vegetables is now being marketed wholesale. The group's aim is a substantial increase in their future vegetable production.

Nurseries

234 We are confident that the relatively recent development of hardy nursery stock production in Argyll and in the Moray Firth area will expand in the future. Production levels are being maintained or increased, despite the depressed wholesale market, linked with financial stringency in local and development authorities, and standards are generally high.

235 Following the successful visit by Highland growers to East Anglian nurseries in 1979, a group of Argyllshire growers made a similar tour in November 1980 with assistance from the board. One of the Argyll group took a stand at the British Growers Look Ahead Exhibition in Harrowgate in 1980. We contributed towards the costs of staging what is now becoming an annual conference for hardy nursery stock growers in the Highlands, held in Oban in October. The conference attracted 140 people from all sections of the trade and stimulated various far-reaching proposals, such as the formation of a national hardy nursery stock association.

236 We terminated our blueberry trial at Conon Bridge in April because of the variable and largely disappointing results obtained over the nine-year period. The project was taken over in its entirety by the owner of the land, allowing us to continue to monitor the economic possibilities of the crop in the future. It is understood that his first year's results have been more encouraging, with the fruit finding a ready local market.

Deer farming

237 In February we were invited to give evidence to a sub-committee of the Farm Animals Welfare Council on welfare aspects of the harvesting of antler velvet from deer. Our written and oral evidence stressed the possible financial

benefits of velvet harvesting while acknowledging the ethical problems raised. On balance we were pleased with the council's recommendation that velveting should be prohibited in the UK.

238 We supported research projects concerned with deer farming. One, carried out by a post-graduate student of Edinburgh University in collaboration with the Hill Farming Research Organisation, is concerned with the measurement of milk production by lactating hinds and the uptake of milk by deer calves. The technique developed will allow precise evaluation of the effects of hind nutrition on the early growth of the calf. A second project, carried out by the Rowett Research Institute, is a detailed study of the anatomy and carcase composition of farmed deer slaughtered at the HFRO farm at Glensaugh. This will give information on the conformation of deer carcases at various stages of growth and on the most efficient means of utilising the farmed deer carcase.

239 We have been encouraged by the increasing interest in deer farming which has seen several new farms being established in the Highlands. To date it has not been our policy to assist the purchase of deer stock in view of the current shortage and the possible consequence on prices. At the end of the year, however, this policy was under review.

240 A group of estates in the Torridon area joined the deer management group scheme during the year. Two other areas also expressed interest. An analysis of cull returns from the mid-Ross area over several years was completed and a report will be produced early in 1981.

241 In 1979 we agreed to support a post-graduate project at Stirling University to examine the market for venison in West Germany, with particular emphasis on the place of Scottish venison. Field work was carried out in Germany during the summer of 1980 when all major importers and processors of venison and a large number of wholesale and institutional buyers were interviewed. A report will be produced by the spring of 1981.

Rahoy deer farm

242 The year saw the final intake of wild deer stock to our deer farm at Rahoy. In addition, a total of 80 calves were born on the farm to our own hinds, the majority to three-year olds. The weights of the calves were very satisfactory but the sex ratio was highly biased in favour of male calves. The reasons for this are not yet clear. Stocking was completed and the herd comprises 404 hinds of all ages and 112 stags. We are now entering the phase in which the large-scale farming system originally envisaged will be evaluated. The first sales of venison and breeding stock should take place during the autumn of 1981.

243 We would like to acknowledge the help we have had from estate stalkers and those of the Red Deer Commission, who

have worked long hours on the hill to catch deer calves for the farm. Without their co-operation and that of estate owners and factors, we could not have achieved our current stock numbers.

244 Development of the farm has progressed with the reseeding of around 80 acres of the lower hill, considerably improving the stocking capacity. The handling system was completed in time for the September gathering, allowing safe and secure handling and sorting of large numbers of deer. Planned fencing of a further substantial area of the upper hill has been deferred following a reappraisal of capital costs on the estate. The farm will continue meantime at its present area of approximately 700 hectares, with attention being redirected to some sub-division of existing sheltered hill-parks.

245 Tourism, based on existing accommodation acquired with Rahoy estate and supplemented by four new chalets, is an important, if subsidiary, revenue earning component of overall management. Although peak season bookings remained at their usual level, there was a noticeable decline in the demand for self-catering accommodation during the shoulder months of 1980 in line with an overall trend throughout the Highlands and Islands. A former storehouse was converted into holiday accommodation in time for the summer season providing 'bunkhouse' style facilities which proved popular with family groups and student parties. One cottage was withdrawn from the list of holiday lettings to provide accommodation for a stockman on the farm.

246 We completed an evaluation of the potential of Loch Teacuis for fish farming and discussions are proceeding with interested parties about the possibilities of setting up a small fish farming unit on the loch.

Muirburn survey

247 This survey, carried out in collaboration with the Nature Conservancy Council and the Game Conservancy, is intended to collect basic data on current muirburn practice on hill and upland farms in west Scotland, on the management of these farms and on the performance of grazing livestock on them. The current work will not, in itself, provide detailed answers to questions about the value of muirburn to grazing stock and on the effects of different practices, but is intended to lay the groundwork for a further stage of investigation. The present work involves interviews and inspections on a sample of around 300 farm units. Field work started in the early summer and by the end of the year just under 100 units had been visited. An advisory panel, chaired by Professor C H Gimingham of Aberdeen University, and comprising representatives of the Institute of Terrestrial Ecology, DAFS, the Hill Farming Research Organisation and the agricultural colleges, has been formed and will meet at intervals during the progress of the survey.

Silage trial

248 To encourage improved fodder production for breeding cattle and sheep, the board supported an investigation into the suitability of baled and bagged silage for Uist conditions. A tractor, baler and operator were made available to interested crofters for two weeks in late July. Nine crofters took part in the trial and made over 120 tons of silage. The North of Scotland College of Agriculture are monitoring the feeding value of the silage over the winter.

Machinery contracting

249 Plans were finalised for a machinery contracting scheme on the Uists. A manure/seaweed spreader, lime/shell sand spreader and grass seed drill will be available for hire on Uist in the spring of 1981. The machinery service will be managed by West Highland Farmers and Crofters Ltd. A larger contracting service for the Ness area in Lewis, to be run by Co-Chomunn Nis Ltd, the multi-functional community co-operative, was at an advanced stage of planning at the end of the year.

Poultry litter

250 Considerable interest has been shown in the past decade in re-cycling poultry manure for feeding to cattle and sheep. Early in 1980 the board contributed towards the cost of a trial which involved feeding ensiled poultry litter to store cattle in an open feed lot. The trial was viewed as a preliminary investigation leading to possible expansion to a 200 head unit. Results were encouraging and in December 1980 the company concerned went ahead to erect slatted courts and storage facilities which will allow the enterprise to get underway in 1981.

Rabbit clearance

251 Since the withdrawal of the Department of Agriculture grants towards rabbit clearance societies, the rabbit population in some islands has increased to such an extent that it is seriously competing for the grazing and cropping requirements of cattle and sheep. The board have assisted communities on Rousay and Colonsay to initiate pilot schemes of comprehensive control, believing that rabbit control can be achieved and maintained within the islands' natural boundaries and where there is total local commitment to the problem. Achievements to date have been partly successful.

Breed societies

252 The board gave assistance towards specific promotional campaigns by the North Country Cheviot Sheep and Beef Shorthorn Societies. Benefits to producers within the Highlands and Islands do arise as a result of the promotions, largely through increased sales of breeding stock for crossing purposes throughout the British Isles and overseas.

Liaison

253 A key feature of the board's work over the years has been close communication and co-operation with many other bodies involved in land development and management. During the year, the advisory committees on Rahoy deer farm, the muirburn survey and the livestock improvement working party provided the board with an impressive wealth of expertise. Many other instances of less formal liaison can

be mentioned, in particular our close involvement with the Highland committee of the National Farmers' Union of Scotland and our support for their strong plea for a special agricultural development programme for the Highlands and Islands on the lines already approved by the EEC for Eire.

254 We value such liaison highly and are indebted to a large number of organisations, including the Department of Agriculture and Fisheries for Scotland, agricultural colleges, Forestry Commission, Crofters Commission, Red Deer Commission, Scottish Agricultural Organisation Society Ltd, Hill Farming Research Organisation, Rowett Research Institute, Macaulay Institute for Soil Research, Meat and Livestock Commission, Nature Conservancy Council, Institute of Terrestrial Ecology, Scottish Horticultural Research Institute, Wool Marketing Board and the milk marketing boards.

Membership and general matters

Membership

255 There was one change in the membership of the board during the year. Mr Thomas C Graham demitted office on 31 October 1980 having served as a part-time member for three years, and in his place the Secretary of State for Scotland appointed Mr Angus S Macdonald for a term of four years from 1 November 1980. The Secretary of State extended the appointment of Mr Robert A Fasken as a full-time member for a further two years to 31 October 1982. At the end of the year membership of the board was therefore as follows:

Sir Kenneth Alexander, chairman
Rear Admiral David A Dunbar-Nasmith, CB, DSC, deputy chairman
Robert A Fasken, CBE
G Gordon Drummond
James Shaw Grant, CBE
Duncan A Ferguson
Angus S Macdonald

Functional responsibilities

256 It was necessary to make some changes to the individual functional responsibilities of full-time members. In addition to his general responsibility for the internal administration of the board and for fishing and fish farming, the deputy chairman assumed control of the implementation of the board's strategy for Hebridean fisheries, thus freeing Mr Drummond to give greater attention to the promotion of the Cromarty Firth area for oil and related developments. Mr Drummond also became responsible for the main stream of industrial development and marketing work. Mr Fasken continued to oversee tourism and land development, while the chairman and secretary remained responsible for policy and research matters and the secretary for financial affairs. Mr Ferguson became the board's nominated director on the board of Lewis Stokfisk Ltd, and was later appointed chairman of the company.

Liaison

257 In addition to his full-time responsibility for the board, the chairman continued to serve on the Scottish Economic Council and on the board of the Scottish Development Agency. Close links at board level were also maintained with the Scottish Tourist Board through Mr Fasken's member-

ship of that body. Towards the end of the year the deputy chairman was appointed to the British Waterways Board. We were particularly pleased about this appointment in view of the importance we attach to the development of the Caledonian and Crinan canals for tourism and other purposes. Mr Drummond continued as chairman of the special programme area board (Highlands and Islands) for the Manpower Services Commission and also as a member of the Cromarty Firth Port Authority.

Meetings

258 The board met fortnightly throughout the year and other meetings were held as necessary to deal with urgent business. A total of 27 meetings were held in 1980 at which 924 applications for financial assistance were considered. Of these, 877 were approved.

Staffing and organisation

259 At the end of the year the staff complement headed by the secretary, Mr J A MacAskill, stood at 249 and was organised on a divisional basis as follows:-

Secretary to board	J A MacAskill
Division	*Head of Division*
Administration	S Edmond (Assistant Secretary)
Finance	D Matheson
Fisheries	J K Lindsay
Industrial development & marketing	J K Farquharson
Land development	H A M MacLean
Policy and research	J T Hughes
Tourism	Dr D A Pattison

260 The preceding chapters of this report give some indication of the volume and growing range of the board's activities. The progress made owes much to the hard work and dedication of our staff at all levels, and we take this opportunity to express our thanks to them. To maintain the effectiveness of staff and to provide opportunities for self-development we have continued to conduct appropriate internal training courses and to send staff to external training courses, seminars and conferences. In addition, younger members of staff have been given day-release facilities to enable them to obtain higher qualifications, and other members of staff have taken advantage of block-release and correspondence courses leading to qualification for membership of professional institutes.

Staff relations

261 During the year the HIDB Whitley Council, chaired by the deputy chairman, met on two occasions to deal with matters concerning conditions of employment, staff relations, accommodation and health and safety at work. We are grateful to those who serve on the staff associations and the Whitley Council and its committees for their contribution to the harmonious working relations within the board.

Legal services

262 Legal services to the board continued to be provided by the office of the Solicitor to the Secretary of State for Scotland, partly by staff seconded to the board's headquarters in Inverness and partly from Scottish Office in Edinburgh.

Finance

263 The board is financed by grant-in-aid borne on the vote of the Scottish Economic Planning Department. Estimated expenditure for the financial period 1 April 1979 to 31 March 1980 was £21 million to be met from estimated receipts of £3,568,000 and grant-in-aid of £17,432,000. The actual expenditure was £21,378,000 which was slightly higher than anticipated. Details of the board's income and expenditure and the balance sheet for the year ended 31 March 1980 are given in Appendix 1 and a statement of receipts and payments in Appendix 3. At a time of severe recession in the national economy and restraint on public expenditure, we wish to record our appreciation to Government for maintaining the level of finance allocated to the board for development.

Directions and proposals

264 No directions of a general character were received from the Secretary of State during the year in terms of Section 2(1) of the Highlands and Islands Development (Scotland) Act 1965. No formal proposal was submitted to the Secretary of State under Section 3(1)(b) of the Act.

Surveys

265 In terms of Section 9(1)(c) of the Act further surveys connected with economic and social developments were carried out during the year using the services of staff, consultants and other agencies. Details are given in the body of the report and in Appendix 6.

Parliamentary Committees

266 During March and April we gave written and supplementary oral evidence to the House of Commons Select Committee on Scottish Affairs who were inquiring into the co-operation and possible overlap among Government departments and statutory authorities and agencies responsible for attracting new investment to Scotland.

267 We stressed to the committee the board's comprehensive approach to economic development and that in the industrial sector most of our promotion and investment was directed to small scale and indigenous industry. It was pointed out, however, that some important successes had been achieved in attracting investment from abroad which would not otherwise have come to the Highlands without a direct board initiative.

268 From the board's point of view, we said that it would be desirable for machinery to be created for co-ordinating inward investment enquiries to Scotland at a Scottish level, and that we were ready to co-operate towards that end. Finally, we stressed the importance we attached to the good links established with the SDA and to the continuation of the arrangement under which a board member was also a member of the SDA board.

269 Later in the year, we gave written and oral evidence to the Committee of Inquiry into Local Government in Scotland. In undertaking our responsibility as the main instrument of Government for stimulating and assisting development in the Highlands and Islands, we maintain close liaison with Government departments and the various local authorities. As regards the structure of local government in the Highlands and Islands, we commented that the three all-purpose island authorities of Shetland, Orkney and the Western Isles had worked well in practice and, at the scale of the operation, seemed to have encountered little difficulty in co-ordinating their various functions. As regards the mainland, we indicated that, on balance, the economic and social development of the Highland mainland could best be progressed by the retention of the two-tier structure, with a strong top-tier strategic planning authority and essentially local matters being dealt with at district level. We thought, however, that the Argyll area, which is part of Strathclyde Region, was so disparate from the urban connurbation of Glasgow that consideration should be given to creating an all-purpose authority covering the present district of Argyll and Bute, Arran and possibly the Cumbraes.

270 On the functions of local government we suggested there was scope for some re-adjustment of powers and function to avoid unnecessary overlap and duplication. We also suggested that there was potential in the Highland mainland area for re-directing the overall local authority input into the development and promotion of tourism. It was felt that the local authority financial contribution to the local servicing of tourism could best be exercised at district level, leaving the regional council to concentrate on the provision of infrastructure and services. As regards recreation and leisure, we felt that there was room for reviewing the provisions of the 1973 Act giving concurrent powers for these functions.

271 Written and oral evidence was also given to the Employment Committee of the House of Commons who were investigating how the work of the Department of Employment and its associated bodies affected different parts of Scotland. Our evidence, which concentrated on industrial training, made the point that the unusual and exceptional economic and geographic conditions of the Highlands, and particularly the islands, made it very difficult for any national schemes of training to cater for the special needs of the area. We said that a need would remain to make provision for the problems of scattered communities and that it was important, therefore, for the board to retain discretion to intervene, in consultation with national agencies as appropriate, to assist in meeting these special needs.

Raasay

272 Following the successful conclusion of protracted negotiations for the purchase of several properties on Raasay, we were able to confirm, early in the year, plans for converting Borodale House into an hotel and to outline further small

development proposals for the island. Public meetings were held on the island to discuss these proposals and to ensure that the community were made aware at first hand of the board's intentions.

The conversion of Borodale House on Raasay into an hotel was well advanced by the end of 1980. It will open for business in the summer of 1981.

273 Included in the proposals was the establishment by a new charitable trust of an adventure training centre to help young people. Part of Raasay House, which is a listed building, will be made available on lease to the trust as the centre's base and living accommodation. We have carried out some repairs to the building, which was largely in a ruinous condition, and the trust themselves have done a good deal of work to rehabilitate the premises. Raasay Home Farm has been retained in hand, and we began work to restore its fertility.

Consultative Council

274 A summary of discussions with the Highlands and Islands Development Consultative Council during the year is given in paragraphs 278 to 289. As indicated in the council's report, a number of important items were remitted to them for advice during the year and the board are grateful for the council's guidance.

Visits and liaison

275 During November, Lord Mansfield, the Minister of State with special responsibility for the Highlands and Islands, visited the board. We welcomed this opportunity to discuss at first hand with the Minister various aspects of the tourism industry in the Highlands and Islands and our plans for adapting to the changing pattern of the industry's needs in our area.

276 We were pleased to receive a number of other distinguished visitors and to help arrange their visits to the Highlands and Islands. Among the visitors to the board's offices in Inverness were Members of Parliament, representatives of the Government of Newfoundland, the Minister for Industrial Development and Decentralisation in New South Wales, the Minister for the Gaeltacht in the Republic of

Ireland, the Moderator of the General Assembly of the Church of Scotland, and a group of members of the European Parliament led by Mrs Winifred Ewing who represents the Highlands and Islands.

277 We have continued to attach great importance to maintaining good liaison with the local authorities in the area and to keeping them informed of the on-going work of the board. We have also kept in close touch with other representative bodies and Government agencies working in the Highlands and Islands. These included the Crofters Commission, the Countryside Commission for Scotland, the Highland Fund, the Nature Conservancy Council, the National Trust for Scotland, the Scottish Development Agency and the Scottish Tourist Board.

Consultative Council

Membership

278 The appointments of the eleven district council nominees expired on 31 July 1980 and new appointments were made for the four year period to 31 July 1984. The Secretary of State also increased to two the number of representatives of each of the Western Isles, Orkney and Shetland authorities in recognition of their all-purpose nature and the geographic disparity of the areas under their administration. These appointments will terminate with those existing for the regional and island authorities on 31 July 1982. The list of members during the year is given at Appendix 7.

Meetings

279 The council continued their practice of holding four meetings during the year. The ad hoc committees held their meetings as required. In May, members of the transport and communications committee, accompanied by the chairman, made a day visit to Mull and Iona. In October the chairman saw a number of board-assisted ventures in Orkney during brief visits to Mainland and Shapinsay.

Land

280 The difficulties caused by the severity of the financial problems in agriculture drew the council's attention throughout the year. The situation was felt to be particularly difficult in the store cattle and sheep sectors, and with increasing production costs, market prices failing to keep pace with inflation, and little immediate prospect of better marketing or improved production techniques providing a solution, Government support was seen as the only method of helping the industry to continue its important role. The board were complimented on the representations they had made to the Minister of State which must have assisted the Government in their decision to introduce further increases in the rates of hill livestock compensatory allowances. In forestry, the council expressed their concern over the need for clarification of Government policy and that leasehold and crofting tenants should be attracted into afforestation schemes in view of the decline in both private and state planting.

281 The council noted and generally agreed with the various recommendations of the report of the Northfield Committee

of Inquiry into the acquisition and occupancy of agricultural land. Disappointment was expressed, however, in the lack of a recommendation about the formation of a land register — an idea that had been urged upon the board for many years. The council were pleased to note the committee appeared to be well disposed towards the board's claim for limited powers of intervention to deal with grossly under-utilised or mis-used land.

Fisheries

282 The report which the board had prepared specially for the council on the development of fish farming was received with considerable interest. Members noted with satisfaction the 56 separate ventures which had attracted financial assistance, and the 57 research and development projects on a variety of fish farming subjects which had been undertaken or commissioned. The board were congratulated on the valuable work done and the expertise acquired in tackling the problems inherent in promoting and developing this comparatively new industry. Acknowledging the crucial role which large companies must play in pioneering the industry, the council suggested nevertheless that ways should be found to involve crofters and local communities in viable fish farming projects, whenever possible.

283 As regards the fishing industry in general, the council registered concern over the effect on the livelihood of Scottish fishermen of high interest rates, the increasing cost of fuel and, in some instances, the subsidies which the governments of some countries were providing in support for their exports. It was felt that these subsidies were putting our own fishermen at a disadvantage in obtaining satisfactory prices for their catches. Keen interest was maintained in the board-supported fish processing venture at Breasclete and, although council members were critical of some aspects of the operation, they congratulated the board on progress to date and on their commitment to ensuring the success of the venture. Favourable comment was made on the Government's proposals to establish a single statutory authority for the fishing industry, and the council endorsed the comments and views expressed by the board regarding the nature and range of functions proposed for the new organisation.

Tourism

284 The council accepted that the decline experienced in tourism during the year was a reflection of the general economic recession. They praised the board for the action they had taken to encourage visitors to come to the Highlands and Islands through promotional marketing schemes both at home and abroad. The need was seen, however, for reviewing the basis of overseas promotion and for better arrangements to be made to bring visitors direct from their overseas locations to the Highlands and Islands. Representations were made strongly to the board that they should firmly resist any suggestion that their responsibility for tourism development in the Highlands and Islands be taken

over by another organisation. The expertise and knowledge built up by the board over the years on the particular needs of their area was seen as vital for success in such a competitive industry and the interest of the Highlands and Islands would be best served by the board continuing and building on their current role.

285 With regard to development in scenic areas, of which twenty-eight in the board's area have been identified as of 'first-class importance' and, having noted the administrative changes proposed whereby the Secretary of State has to be notified of planning applications and local planning authorities obliged to consult the Countryside Commission for Scotland, the council supported the reservations formally expressed by the board in response to a consultative document issued by the Scottish Development Department. Although they accepted that development policy must necessarily be influenced by many agencies, members showed particular concern that undue influence might be applied by bodies based outwith the Highlands and Islands and which had no prime concern for economic factors. The council strongly urged the board to undertake a review of the increasing encroachment upon scenic areas by conservation bodies, paying particular attention to the extent to which the designation of areas as nature reserves would exclude visitors and could inhibit desirable economic development.

Industry

286 The council shared the disappointment felt by the board at the closure of the pulp mill at Fort William with its economic impact on the Lochaber area. At the outset of the board's activity, Lochaber had been seen as a natural growth point, and council members were concerned that the impact of the closure would go beyond its immediate effect and add to a cumulative weakening of the economic and social fabric of the area. The council praised the board on their efforts to save the employment at the pulp mill and in launching the special job creation project aimed at attracting new jobs for the already unemployed and for those who may be affected through lay-offs in other industries.

287 On the prospect of petrochemical development in the Cromarty/Moray Firth area the council, through representation to the board, emphasised the importance to the nation and the Highlands and Islands generally of a Government decision that would unequivocally establish the availability of feedstock, including ethane, at Nigg Bay before the end of the decade, preferably with assured availability by 1986. It was seen as essential that a pipeline from St Fergus to Nigg be accepted as an integral part of the gas gathering system and crucial for the Government to create a framework within which companies competing for an opportunity to establish at Nigg might negotiate price and quantity of a supply of ethane so that the successful company would have a firm contractual basis for any future planning. The importance of such petrochemical develop-

ment was underlined both in the short term as an employment generator for many British capital goods industries and in the medium term as a means of maximising the gain to the British economy from adding value to North Sea gas.

General

288 The agenda at each of the council's quarterly meetings has included a report on the board's work and members have expressed their appreciation to the board for these detailed reports and for the amplification which board members and staff have given in discussion.

289 Other main topics covered at the council's meetings during the year have been the principles and formation of community co-operatives, social research, transport issues (including the operation of road equivalent tariff and the future of sea ferries), the economic effects of by-passing communities by road improvement, the concurrent functions of public authorities in the Highland Region, electricity tariffs in the North of Scotland and petrol supplies in the Highlands and Islands. Additionally, the council have offered advice to the board in consideration of various official inquiries and investigations, including the House of Commons Select Committee on Employment, the Committee of Inquiry into Local Government in Scotland, and the House of Lords European Communities Committee Inquiry into EEC Regional Policy.

Appendices

Statement of accounting policies

Appendix 1

Statement 1

1 **Basis of accounting**

(a) The accounts have been prepared under the historical cost convention in a form determined by the Secretary of State for Scotland with the approval of Treasury in accordance with section 13 of the Highlands and Islands Development (Scotland) Act 1965.

(b) The accounts have been prepared on a basis which takes account of the board's functions and objectives and which, without limiting the information given, meets the requirements of the Companies Acts 1948 to 1976 and of the Statements of Standard Accounting Practice issued by the accounting bodies represented on the Consultative Committee of Accountancy Bodies so far as these requirements are appropriate to the board.

(c) The accounts of the board's 75 per cent subsidiary, Lewis Stokfisk Ltd., are shown as an appendix to these accounts, but have not been audited by the Comptroller and Auditor General. In the board's opinion none of the minority investments conform to the definition of associated companies contained in the Statement of Standard Accounting Practice. Consolidated accounts have not been prepared because the nature and diversity of the board's operations and those of their invested companies preclude meaningful accounts in that form.

2 **Funding**

The board receive grant-in-aid from the Secretary of State to finance their capital expenditure and the excess of their revenue expenditure over attributable income. The board account for the grant-in-aid funds received in this way by a credit to their general fund. A transfer is then made from the income and expenditure account to the general fund of an amount equal to the board's net revenue expenditure.

3 **Fixed assets and depreciation**

(a) Fixed assets are shown at cost less depreciation. As from this year depreciation on buildings will commence in the year in which a certificate of practical completion is received.

(b) No depreciation is provided on land, site development work and buildings under construction. All other fixed assets are depreciated on a straight line basis having regard to their estimated operating lives and anticipated residual values. The annual rates of depreciation are 2 per cent of buildings, 10 per cent of plant and equipment, and 25 per cent on vehicles.

4 **Investments and loans**

Investments are shown at cost less provision for any diminution in value in the opinion of the board. Loans are shown at the amount outstanding at balance sheet date less provision for estimated losses where the board consider that loans may not be recovered in full.

5 **Bad debts**

Bad and doubtful debts are written off at the earliest opportunity. Provision is made for debts which the board consider are unlikely to be recovered but which have not yet been written off.

6 **Accruals**

The accruals in respect of loan interest shown in these accounts reflect only those debts for which demands had been issued as at 31 March 1980.

Income and expenditure account

Appendix 1
Statement 2

for the year ended 31 March 1980

Previous Year (restated) £'000	INCOME	£'000	£'000
838	Loan and debenture interest		1,013
173	Income from leased assets		181
63	Income from board projects		91
41	Grants repaid		132
184	Other receipts		169
1,299			1,586
	Less: EXPENDITURE		
4,103	Grant assistance	4,582	
2,134	Administration costs (note 1)	2,572	
1,058	Research, surveys and publicity	890	
1,182	Projects and development schemes (note 2)	1,380	
8,477			9,424
7,178			7,838
254	Depreciation	384	
27	(Profit)/Loss on disposal of assets and investments	(44)	
335	Provision for bad debts and losses on investments (note 3)	782	
185	Investments and other bad debts written off	69	
15	Interest written off	6	
816			1,197
	EXCESS OF EXPENDITURE OVER INCOME		
7,994	Transferred to general fund, financed by grant-in-aid		9,035

Balance Sheet

Appendix 1

Statement 3

as at 31 March 1980

Previous Year £'000		£'000	£'000
	ASSETS EMPLOYED:		
8,688	Fixed assets (statement 6)		13,062
1,491	Investments (unquoted) (note 4)		1,480
13,439	Loans (note 5)		17,314
	CURRENT ASSETS:		
457	Debtors	508	
9	Cash and bank balances	9	
466		517	
589	Creditors and accruals	481	
(123)	Net current assets		36
23,495			31,892
	FINANCED BY:		
	General Fund		
18,789	Balance, 1 April 1979		23,495
12,700	Grant-in-aid received during year		17,432
31,489			40,927
7,994	Excess of expenditure over income for year		9,035
23,495			31,892

The notes in statements 5 and 6 form part of these accounts

KJW Alexander
Accounting Officer

11 November 1980

Statement of source and application of funds

Appendix 1
Statement 4

for year ended 31 March 1979

Previous Year (Restated) £'000		£'000	£'000
	SOURCE OF FUNDS:		
12,700	From H M Exchequer: Grant-in-aid		17,432
	Funds from other sources:		
1,674	Repayment of loans	2,225	
176	Proceeds from sale of assets and investments	166	
1,850			2,391
14,550			19,823
	APPLICATION OF FUNDS:		
7,994	Excess of expenditure over income		9,035
	Adjustment for items not involving movement of funds:		
62	Income recoverable in previous years now written off	21	
(254)	Depreciation	(384)	
(27)	Profit/(loss) on disposal of assets and investments	44	
(335)	Provision for bad debts and losses on investments	(782)	
(185)	Investments and other bad debts written off	(69)	
(15)	Interest written off	(6)	
(754)			(1,176)
7,240			7,859
4,517	Loans made	6,470	
2,681	Purchase of fixed assets	4,820	
330	Investments made	463	
7,528			11,753
14,768			19,612
(218)	INCREASE/(DECREASE) IN WORKING CAPITAL:		211
178	Debtors		103
(324)	Creditors		108
(72)	Cash in hand at bank		—
(218)			211

Notes on the accounts

Appendix 1
Statement 5

1 ADMINISTRATION COSTS

	1979-80	*1978-79*
(1) Salaries, superannuation, etc.:	£'000	*£'000*
Board members	72	*52*
Staff	1,746	*1,420*
	1,818	*1,472*

The chairman's remuneration was £17,819.98 (*£12,422*).

The deputy chairman and two full-time board members' salaries ranged between £10,000 and £15,000.

No staff member's remuneration exceeded £20,000.

(2) Travelling and subsistence:	£'000	*£'000*
Board members	20	*21*
Staff	222	*201*
	242	*222*
(3) General administration expenses	£'000	*£'000*
Rent and rates	129	*108*
Telephone and postage	100	*88*
Legal fees and expenses	78	*63*
Equipment and furnishing (non-capital)	66	*68*
Others	112	*94*
	485	*421*
(4) Audit fee	£'000	*£'000*
	20	*11*
(5) Consultative Council	£'000	*£'000*
	7	*8*
	£'000	*£'000*
Total administration costs	2,572	*2,134*

2 PROJECTS & DEVELOPMENT SCHEMES REVENUE EXPENDITURE

	1979-80	*1978-79*
	£'000	*£'000*
Area tourist organisations	303	*264*
Training schemes	185	*167*
Board property factoring costs	145	*116*
Community co-op schemes	126	*48*
Highland Craftpoint	117	*5*
Rahoy Estate	108	*80*
Moniack fish farm	39	*37*
Others	357	*465*
	1,380	*1,182*

3 PROVISION FOR LOSSES

The movements in the provision are as follows:—

	Investments	Loan Capital & Interest*	Others
	£'000	£'000	£'000
Provision as at 1 April 1979	400	450	20
Provision for year	410	350	22
Provision as at 31 March 1981	810	800	42

*Included in the provision at 31 March 1980 is loan interest of £30,000

4 INVESTMENTS (UNQUOTED)

	Ordinary Pref Ord	Preference Shares	Debentures	Total
	£'000	£'000	£'000	£'000
Balance at 1 April 1979	1,505	348	38	1,891
Additions during year	318	145	—	463
	1,823	493	38	2,354
Amount written off	8	—	—	8
	1,815	493	38	2,346
Shareholding sold	56	—	—	56
	1,759	493	38	2,290
Provision for losses				810
				1,480

There were equity commitments at 31 March 1980 amounting to £183,00 *(£368,000)* in respect of seven (14) companies.

Of the five investments sold during the year a profit of £32,000 was made in one case and a loss of £16,000 was made in three cases. The other investment was sold at cost.

The board have a majority investment in Lewis Stokfisk Ltd. as follows:—

	1980	*1979*
	£'000	*£'000*
300,000 £1 Ordinary shares (representing 75 per cent of the voting rights)	300	*300*
100,000 £1 Preference shares	100	*100*
	400	*400*

The unquoted minority investments represent holdings in the following 53 companies:
Ordinary and preferred ordinary shares:

- Acair Ltd
- Ardanaisaig Hotel Ltd
- Barguillean Nurseries Ltd
- Barratlantic Ltd
- Breasclete Fishing Co Ltd
- Bute Fabrics Ltd
- Cairngorm Chairlift Co Ltd
- Caithness Glass Ltd
- Caley Cruisers Ltd
- Clansman Holdings Ltd
- Computacomp (UK) Ltd
- J. & M. Crawford (Inverdruie) Ltd
- Dalriada Hotels (Tarbert) Ltd
- Esplanade West (Oban) Ltd
- Gaelspun Ltd
- Gairloch Construction Ltd
- Gairloch Seafoods Ltd
- Hebridean Knitwear Ltd
- Highland Fish Farmers Ltd
- Highland Heathers Ltd
- Highland Music Co Ltd
- Highland Trout Co (Scotland) Ltd
- Inverliever Nurseries Ltd
- Jacobite Cruises Ltd
- John F. Munro (Contractors) Ltd
- D. A. Johnson (North Uist) Ltd
- Kintyre Data Processing Ltd
- Lomar Holidays Ltd
- Norman MacKenzie (Building Supplies) Ltd
- W. J. MacLeod (Fishing) Ltd
- Machrie Developments Ltd
- Maricult Flotation Ltd
- Manor Hotel (Stornoway) Ltd
- Muileann Beag a'Chrotail Ltd
- Norfrost Ltd
- Norscot Hotels Ltd
- Northern Lights Investments Ltd
- Orcantic Ltd
- Otter Ferry Salmon Ltd
- Rotary Precision Ltd
- Scottish Sea Farms Ltd
- Seabear Seafoods Ltd
- Seaforth Hotel (Stornoway) Ltd
- Shetland Norse Preserving Co Ltd
- Stags Head Hotel (Fort William) Ltd
- Strathspey Railway Co Ltd
- Tanmoor Hotel Ltd
- Thaneway Ltd
- Tobermory Distillers Ltd
- Underwater Trials Ltd
- Vu Data Ltd
- Wester Ross Salmon Ltd
- Whiteness Development Co Ltd

In all cases the ordinary share investment represents less than 40 per cent of the voting rights of the company concerned.

Preference Shares:

- Alexander Robertson & Sons (Yacht Builders) Ltd
- Borrodale Hotel (South Uist) Ltd
- Campbeltown Shipyard Ltd
- Computacomp (UK) Ltd
- John G. Eccles (Printers) Ltd
- Elanders Ltd
- Fort William (Cruachan Hotel) Ltd
- Gairloch Seafoods Ltd
- Grampian Records Ltd
- Highland Universal Fabrications Ltd
- Norman MacKenzie (Building Supplies) Ltd
- Norfrost Ltd
- Norscot Hotels Ltd
- Orcantic Ltd
- Osprey Electronics Ltd
- Rotary Precision Ltd
- Skye Marble Ltd
- Stags Head Hotel (Fort William) Ltd
- Tanmoor Hotel Ltd
- Wester Ross Salmon Ltd

Debentures:

- Cairngorm Chairlift Co Ltd

5 LOANS	£'000	£'000
Balance, 1 April 1979	13,889	
Additions	6,470	20,359
Repayments	2,225	
Amounts written off	50	
		2,275
		18,084
Provision		770
		17,314

6 There were commitments amounting to £8.1m (1979: £10.1m) in respect of grant and loan assistance to be provided under the board's scheme of grants and loans. In addition, there were commitments of £4.1m (1979: £5.2m) in respect of board properties.

7 During the year ended 31 March 1980, grant recoverable of £26,000 (1979: £87,000) in four (eleven) cases was written off.

8 The board's superannuation scheme does not provide for increased pensions under the Pension's Increase Act 1971 and any increase due to be paid to members of the scheme or their dependants under this Act would fall to be met by the the board from their grant in aid.

9 Rent free concessions during the year amount to £128,000 (1979: £31,000) in nineteen cases — this included a sum of £52,000 in respect of Lewis Stokfisk.

10 A claim was abandoned of £21,534.90 against Charles Black Ltd, Dunoon in respect of the year ended 31 March 1979.

11 During the year the board paid from grant in aid a sum of £22,932.60 to an employee as compensation for loss of office. In addition, an annual compensation payment of £1,816.67 is payable until December 1994. The board's superannuation scheme is a funded insurance scheme, and does not contain provisions for this type of payment. The payments were based on analogous Civil Service conditions of service which the board is required to apply throughout. An error was made in not obtaining prior Treasury approval. These sums were retrospectively approved by Treasury.

12 It has been the board's practice to charge to the income and expenditure account the costs and sales proceeds of publications. Unsold stocks held by the board at 31 March 1980 which were not treated as assets in the accounts were valued at £108,000 on the basis of selling price to retailers, but some of the publications are out of date and the net realisable value was very much lower than this. The board intend to discontinue production of commercial type publications for resale.

CERTIFICATE AND REPORT OF THE COMPTROLLER AND AUDITOR GENERAL

I have examined the foregoing balance sheet and income and expenditure account and the supporting information set out in the statement of accounting policies, the statement of source and application of funds and the notes. These have been prepared under the historical cost convention and comply with the provisions of the Highlands and Islands Development (Scotland) Act 1965 and determinations made thereunder by the Secretary of State.

I certify that in my opinion the balance sheet, income and expenditure account and supporting information give, under the accounting convention stated above, a true and fair view of the state of affairs of the Highlands and islands Development Board at 31 March 1980 and of its results and the source and application of its funds for the year ended on that date. I have no observations to make upon these accounts.

Douglas Henley
Comptroller and Auditor General

Exchequer and Audit Department
23 December 1980

Fixed assets — Property

Appendix 1

Statement 6

	Property leased out						Other Property				
	Land	Factories	Hotels	Area Tourist Offices	Others	Raasay	Fish Hatchery	Deer Farm	Admin. Use	Equipment and Vehicles	Total
	£'000	£'000	£'000	£'000	£'000	£'000	£'000	£'000	£'000	£'000	£'000
COST											
Balance, 1 April 1979	562	5,260	779	309	787	—	49	332	36	1,199	9,313
Acquisitions during year	158	3,757	86	172	264	155	—	76	—	152	4,820
	720	9,017	865	481	1,051	155	49	408	36	1,351	14,133
Disposal (gross) during year	1	50	—	—	—	—	—	—	—	53	104
As at 31 March 1980	719	8,967	865	481	1,051	155	49	408	36	1,298	14,029
DEPRECIATION											
As at 31 March 1979	—	141	43	16	48	—	8	17	4	348	625
Addition for 1979-80	—	175	16	8	17	3	1	6	—	158	384
Disposals	—	(2)	—	—	—	—	—	—	—	(40)	(42)
As at 31 March 1980	—	314	59	24	65	3	9	23	4	466	967
Written down values as at 31 March 1980	719	8,653	806	457	986	152	40	385	32	832	13,062
Written down values as at 31 March 1979	562	5,119	736	293	739	—	41	315	32	851	8,688

Expendinture on assets under construction of £820,923 is included in the cost as at 31 March 1980 figure of the total written down value.
Of £13,062,303 as at 31 March 1980 the sum of £1,348,029 relates to leasehold property.

Lewis Stokfisk Limited
Statement of accounting policies

Appendix 2
Statement 1

DEPRECIATION

Depreciation is provided in equal annual instalments over the estimated useful life of the assets and is calculated on cost of the asset. An appropriate proportion of the annual charge is provided in the year of acquisition.

The following rates are used:

Plant and equipment:	15%
Motor vehicles:	25%

FOREIGN CURRENCIES

Adjustments due to currency fluctuations in the normal course of business are included in the trading deficit.

GOVERNMENT GRANTS

Government grants receivable in respect of capital expenditure are credited to a special account and are released to the profit and loss account over the estimated lives of the assets to which they relate.

INVENTORIES

Inventories are stated at the lower of cost (on a first in first out basis) and net realisable value. Cost represents all direct costs incurred in bringing inventories to their present state and location.

ASSOCIATED COMPANY

An associated company is a company other than a subsidiary in which the company's interest is considered to be long-term and is at least 20 per cent of the equity voting rights of the company. The profit and loss account includes the company's share of the trading results of the associated company and the balance sheet liability comprises the company's share of the associated company's post acquisition deficit less the acquistion price of the shares.

Lewis Stokfisk Limited

Appendix 2
Statement 2

Profit and loss account
Year ended 31 December 1979

	1979		*31 Oct. 1977 to 31 Dec. 1979*
	£	£	£
TURNOVER		290,415	*18,342*
TRADING LOSS		308,649	77,794
After crediting:			
Interest received	—		*11,688*
Capital grants release	41,903		*3,207*
and after charging:			
Depreciation	87,973		*7,230*
Auditors' remuneration	2,000		*1,000*
Interest on bank overdraft	33,082		*524*
Director's emoluments	—		—
Share of loss of associated company		33,104	—
		341,753	*77,794*
TAXATION (note 1)		3,019	—
LOSS ATTRIBUTABLE TO THE SHAREHOLDERS OF LEWIS STOKFISK LIMITED		344,772	*77,794*
Deficit at 1 January 1979		77,794	—
ACCUMULATED DEFICIT AT 31 December 1979 (Note 2)		422,566	*77,794*

The statement of accounting policies at statement 1 and notes at statement 5 form part of these accounts.

Lewis Stokfisk Limited

Appendix 2

Statement 3

Balance sheet

31 December 1979

	Note	1979 £	1979 £	*1978* *£*
CAPITAL EMPLOYED				
Share capital	3		500,000	*500,000*
(Deficit)	4		(322,566)	*22,206*
SHAREHOLDERS' FUNDS			177,434	*522,206*
Long term loans	5		250,000	—
Capital grants			237,454	*252,093*
			£664,888	*£774,299*
REPRESENTED BY				
Fixed assets	6		547,595	*566,174*
Associated company	7		(13,104)	*20,000*
			534,491	*586,174*
Current assets:				
Inventories	8	51,642		*79,795*
Capital grants receivable		77,132		*255,300*
Debtors		40,128		*38,222*
Taxation recoverable		1,494		—
Cash		3		*3*
		170,399		*373,320*
Current liabilities:				
Creditors		37,396		*65,125*
Bank overdraft (secured)		2,606		*120,070*
		40,002		*185,195*
Net current assets			130,397	*188,125*
			£664,888	*£774,299*

JOHN ANGUS, Director
PER G STOKNES, Director

The statement of accounting policies at statement 1 and notes at statement 5 form part of these accounts.

Lewis Stokfisk Limited

Appendix 2

Statement 4

Statement of source and application of funds

Year ended 31 December 1979

	1979	*13 Oct. 1977 to 31 Dec. 1978*
	£	£
SOURCE OF FUNDS		
Issue of share capital	—	*500,000*
Loan	250,000	—
Highlands and Islands Development Board special grant	—	*100,000*
Regional development and FEOGA grants	205,432	—
	455,432	*600,000*
APPLICATION OF FUNDS		
Loss for year	308,649	*77,794*
Adjustment of items not involving the movement of funds:		
Depreciation	87,973	*7,230*
Capital grants release	41,903	*3,207*
	46,070	*4,023*
Net outflow through operations	262,579	*73,771*
Purchases of fixed assets	69,394	*573,404*
Corporation tax paid	4,513	—
Investment in associate company	—	*20,000*
	£336,486	*667,175*
INCREASE IN WORKING CAPITAL	118,946	*67,175*
CHANGES IN WORKING CAPITAL		
Increase (decrease) in inventories	(28,153)	*79,795*
Increase in debtors	1,906	*38,222*
Increase in cash	—	*3*
Decrease (increase) in creditors	27,729	*(65,125)*
Decrease (increase) in bank overdraft	117,464	*(120,070)*
	£118,946	*£(67,175)*

Lewis Stokfisk Limited

Appendix 2

Statement 5

Notes on the accounts

	1979 £	1978 £
1 TAXATION		
Lewis Stokfisk Limited — underprovision for previous year	3,019	—

There are tax losses of £812,000 carried forward

	1979 £	1978 £
2 ACCUMULATED DEFICIT		
The accumulated deficit is dealt with in the accounts of:		
Lewis Stokfisk Limited	389,462	*77,794*
Associated company	33,104	—
	422,566	*77,794*
3 SHARE CAPITAL		
Authorised, issued and fully paid:		
100,000 15% redeemable non-cumulative preference shares of £1 each		
400,000 ordinary shares of £1 each	100,000	*100,000*
400,000 ordinary shares of £1 each	400,000	*400,000*
	500,000	*500,000*

The preference shares are redeemable at any time using profits or monies of the company which may be lawfully applied for the redemption of preference shares at par.

	1979 £	1978 £
4 DEFICIT		
Highlands and Islands Development Board special grant	100,000	*100,000*
(Accumulated trading deficit)	(422,566)	*(77,794)*
	(322,566)	*22,206*

The accumulated trading deficit includes £33,104 (1978-nil) relating to the associated company.

5 LONG TERM LOANS

The loans from the Highlands and Islands Development Board comprise a working capital loan of £150,000,bearing interest at 10 per cent per annum from 23 August 1980, and repayable in five equal instalments commencing 23 August 1981 and a plant and machinery loan, bearing interest at 10 per cent per annum from 23 August 1981 and repayable in eight equal instalments commencing 23 August 1982. The terms of the repayment of this latter loan are subject to review on 23 August 1984.

Notes on the accounts

6 FIXED ASSETS

	Plant £	*Vehicles* £	*Total* £
COST			
At 1 January 1979	565,930	7,474	*573,404*
Additions	69,394	—	*69,394*
At 31 December 1979	635,324	7,474	*642,798*
DEPRECIATION			
At 1 January 1979	7,074	156	*7,230*
Charge for year	86,105	1,868	*87,973*
At 31 December 1979	93,179	2,024	*95,203*
NET BOOK AMOUNT			
At 31 December 1979	542,145	5,450	*547,595*
At 31 December 1978	558,856	7,318	*566,174*

FUTURE CAPITAL EXPENDITURE

	1979 £	*1978* £
No provision has been made in these accounts for:		
Expenditure for which contracts have been placed	Nil	*Nil*
Other authorised expenditure for which no contracts have been placed	Nil	*45,000*

7 ASSOCIATED COMPANY

	1979 £	*1978* £
Unquoted investment at cost to the company (directors' valuation Nil: *1978 £20,000)*	20,000	*20,000*
Share attributable deficit	(33,104)	—
	£(13,104)	*£20,000*

At 31 December 1979 the following company was considered and associated company:

	Country of Registration	% Equity Voting Rights
Breasclete Fishing Company Limited	Scotland	40

8 INVENTORIES

	1979 £	1978 £
Raw materials	22,664	*43,709*
Consumables	14,597	*12,517*
Finished goods	14,381	*23,569*
	51,642	*£79,795*

Auditors Report

To the members of Lewis Stokfisk Limited

We have examined the accounts set out which have been prepared under the historical cost convention.

In our opinion these accounts give, under that convention, a true and fair view of the state of affairs at 31 December 1979 and of the loss and source and application of funds of the company for the year ended 31 December 1979, and comply with the Companies Acts 1948 and 1967.

Mann Judd
Chartered Accountants

19 June 1980

26 Lewis Street
Stornoway
Isle of Lewis
PA87 2JF

Grant in aid account

Appendix 3

for the year ended 31 March 1980

RECEIPTS	£
Balance 1 April 1979	9,233
Grant in aid (Estimate £17,432.000)	17,432,000
Other receipts (Estimate 3,568,000)	£3,946,193 (a)
	£21,387,426

PAYMENTS	£	£
1 Salaries etc (Estimate £1,840,000)		1,820,794
2 Travelling and subsistence (Estimate £245,000)		247,630
3 General administration expenses (Estimate £507,000)		525,979
4 Consultative Council (Estimate £8,000)		7,694
Research, surveys, publicity etc (Estimate £1,050,000)		1,002,139
6 Grants and loans to industry etc (Estimate £11,000,000)		
Grants and loans	11,052,799	
Acquisition of equities	463,000	11,515,799
7 Projects and development schemes (Estimate £6,350,000)		6,258,389
Balance 31 March 1980		9,002
		21,387,426

*The income and expenditure account and balance sheet of the board are published seperately as a White Paper

Explanation of the causes of variations between estimates and actual
(a) Receipts higher than anticipated.

K J W Alexander, Accounting Officer

HIDB Statistical areas

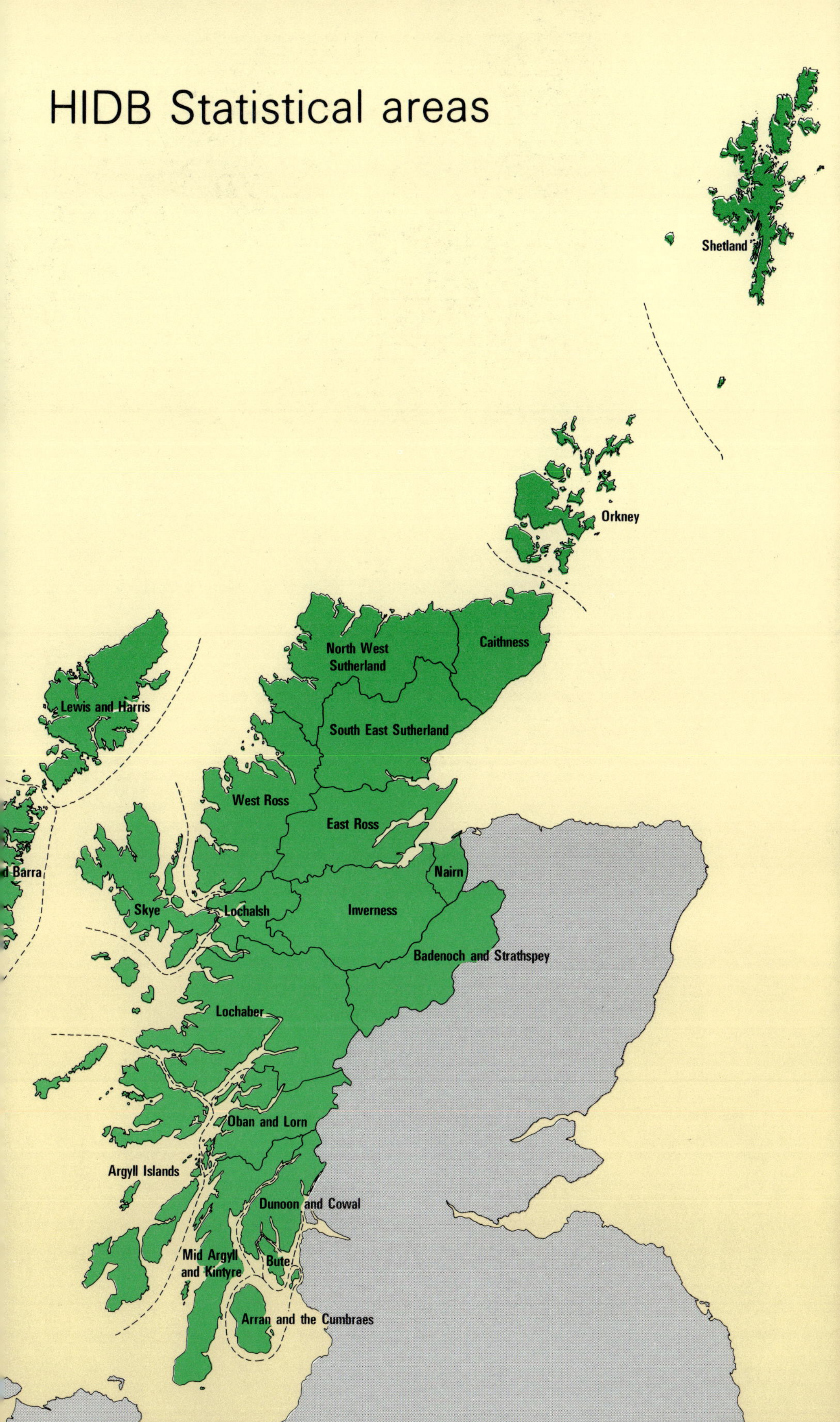

Population

Table 1 Appendix 4

1921-1971 by statistical area and population as % of 1961 total

	1921	%	1931	%	1951	%	1961	%	1971	%
Shetland	25,520	143	21,421	120	19,352	109	17,812	100	17,567	99
Orkney	24,111	129	22,077	118	21,255	113	18,747	100	17,254	92
Caithness	28,285	103	25,656	94	22,710	83	27,370	100	27,915	102
NW Sutherland	6,998	177	5,791	146	4,283	108	3,961	100	3,782	95
SE Sutherland	11,858	116	11,272	110	10,130	99	10,245	100	10,100	98
West Ross and Lochalsh	9,633	142	8,599	126	7,321	108	6,807	100	6,809	100
Lochalsh									2,361	
East Ross	31,753	113	28,033	99	28,713	102	28,199	100	30,480	108
Inverness	38,194	83	40,046	87	45,620	100	45,820	100	49,468	108
Nairn	8,790	104	8,294	98	8,719	104	8,423	100	8,304	99
Badenoch	10,944	120	9,732	107	9,497	104	9,093	100	9,099	100
Skye	11,607	149	10,407	134	8,632	111	7,772	100	7,481	96
Lewis and Harris	33,654	133	29,673	118	27,722	110	25,222	100	23,702	94
Lewis	28,378	129	25,205	115	23,731	108	21,937	100	20,739	95
Harris	5,276	161	4,468	136	3,991	122	3,285	100	2,963	90
Uists and Barra	10,523	143	9,313	126	7,869	107	7,387	100	6,765	92
Lochaber	11,426	80	13,198	93	13,783	97	14,236	100	17,597	124
Ardnamurchan	2,497	167	2,108	141	1,779	119	1,493	100	1,500	100
Argyll Islands	12,356	159	10,537	136	8,849	114	7,772	100	7,480	96
Oban and Lorn	16,020	106	15,202	100	14,615	96	15,162	100	15,078	99
Mid Argyll and Kintyre	21,628	116	19,420	104	20,217	108	18,716	100	18,564	99
Dunoon and Cowal	24,361	150	15,780	97	17,901	110	16,247	100	16,772	103
Bute	19,465	199	12,126	124	12,548	128	9,799	100	8,429	86
Arran and the Cumbraes	14,246	266	6,697	125	6,725	126	5,359	100	4,886	91
HIDB Area	371,372	122	323,277	106	316,471	104	304,161	100	307,532	101

Source: Census of Population.

Population Change

Table 2 Appendix 4

1971-1980 by local authority areas *(see pages 28 and 29 for map)*

Area	1971 Population	1974 Population	1979 Population	1980 Population	Natural Increase 74-80	Est. Net migration 74-80	Other[1] Changes 74-80	% Change per annum 1971-80
HIGHLAND[2]	170,375	178,368	190,507	191,188	+1,671	+8,485	+2,664	+1.29
Caithness[2]	27,779	27,901	27,021	27,033	+141	-966	-43	-0.30
Sutherland[2]	13,634	13,410	13,217	13,168	-319	-309	+386	-0.39
Ross and Cromarty	34,600	38,226	44,502	44,720	+1,309	+5,015	+170	+2.89
Skye and Lochalsh[2]	9,644	9,759	10,031	10,121	-267	+287	+342	+0.54
Lochaber[2]	18,674	19,226	20,150	19,962	+311	-357	+782	+0.74
Inverness	49,004	51,897	55,721	56,407	+614	+3,569	+327	+1.58
Badenoch and Strathspey	8,736	9,043	9,457	9,386	-83	-21	+447	+0.80
Nairn	8,304	8,906	10,408	10,391	-35	+1,267	+253	+2.52
ORKNEY	17,137	17,462	18,134	18,030	-55	+618	+5	+0.57
SHETLAND	17,535	18,445	22,111	22,309	+438	+3,687	-261	+2.71
WESTERN ISLES	30,327	30,060	29,758	29,681	-401	+189	-167	-0.24
Argyll and Bute[2]	62,957	64,578	64,262	64,286	-1,137	+653	+192	+0.23
HIDB AREA (Excluding Arran and the Cumbraes)	298,331	308,913	324,772	325,494	+516	+13,632	+2,433	+0.97

NOTES:

1—'Other changes' encompass Forces movements, etc. and any adjustments made to the base year population by the General Register Office to account for more accurate information not available for that year's population estimate calculations.

2—The 1971 and 1974 figures for these areas have been adjusted by the HIDB to make them comparable with the 1979 and 1980 figures which take account of the following boundary changes since the reorganisation of local government:—

(a) part of the parish of Glenelg has been transferred from the Lochaber District to the Skye and Lochalsh District of Highland Region;
(b) the parishes of Tongue and Farr have been transferred from the Caithness District to the Sutherland District of Highland Region;
(c) Part of the parishes of Lismore and Appin, Ardchattan and Muckairn and Glenorchy and Inishail have been transferred from the Argyll and Bute District of Strathclyde Region to the Lochaber District of Highland Region.

Source: General Register Office, Scotland.

Employment exchange areas

Unemployment by employment exchange area

1971, 1979 and 1980

	MALES (%)			FEMALES (%)			TOTAL (%)		
	1971	1979	1980	1971	1979	1980	1971	1979	1980
Lerwick	6.4	3.2	2.8	2.6	2.9	3.2	5.1	3.0	2.9
Kirkwall	5.7	6.4	8.2	2.2	5.3	6.1	4.5	6.1	7.4
Thurso	6.5	10.9	8.6	6.8	13.1	12.0	6.6	11.5	9.6
Wick	13.8	11.3	13.2	6.5	11.5	8.6	11.1	11.3	11.1
Dingwall/Invergordon	12.7	9.8	10.2	4.6	16.5	12.7	10.0	11.4	11.1
Inverness	7.5	8.4	8.3	2.2	5.9	5.9	5.5	7.5	7.4
Nairn	9.4	12.1	14.0	3.3	7.7	9.0	6.8	10.4	11.9
Portree	13.4	21.6	20.8	2.7	11.9	11.5	9.1	18.1	17.2
Stornoway	28.3	17.4	18.6	9.0	8.0	8.1	22.1	14.0	14.7
Fort William	5.4	6.6	7.9	5.1	8.9	9.4	5.3	7.4	8.5
Oban	10.7	9.9	9.5	4.0	6.6	7.1	7.9	8.4	8.5
Lochgilphead	5.1	8.8	7.9	3.8	6.2	7.6	4.7	7.7	7.8
Campbeltown	13.0	12.0	12.4	9.2	10.7	12.3	11.6	11.5	12.4
Dunoon	7.2	4.5	7.7	3.2	6.9	8.8	5.3	5.2	8.1
Rothesay	9.3	20.4	18.3	2.4	8.4	9.5	6.2	14.9	14.4
TOTAL HIDB AREA (excl. Arran & the Cumbraes)	10.0	9.4	9.8	4.2	8.2	8.0	7.9	9.0	9.1
SCOTLAND	7.5	9.1	11.3	2.9	6.6	8.2	5.7	8.0	10.0
GREAT BRITAIN	4.8*	6.6	8.5	1.5*	4.2	5.5	3.5*	5.6	7.3

*Includes temporarily stopped

Source: Manpower Services Commission

Structure of employment

Table 4 Appendix 4

(excluding proprietors and self-employed)

	H & I June 1971 Male	H & I June 1971 Female	H & I June 1971 Total	H & I June 1977 Male	H & I June 1977 Female	H & I June 1977 Total	June 1977 H & I %	June 1977 Scotland %	June 1977 Britain %
Agriculture[2]									
Forestry	5550	800	6300	4800	700	5500	4.6	2.0	1.6
Fishing[3]	1600	150	1750	1300	150	1450	1.2	0.2	0.1
Mining & Quarrying	3050	10	3100	3150	20	3200	2.7	0.1	—
TOTAL PRIMARY	400	10	400	550	20	600	0.5	1.7	1.6
Grain Milling, Bread, Biscuits, etc.	10602	939	11541	9807	872	10679	8.9	4.1	3.3
Bacon Curing, Meat & Fish Products	450	200	600	400	200	600	0.5	1.0	0.7
Milk & Dairy Products	750	450	1250	600	500	1100	0.9	0.9	0.5
Miscellaneous Food Industries and Tobacco	300	150	450	300	150	450	0.4	0.2	0.2
Drink Industries	100	20	150	100	50	200	0.2	0.6	1.1
Coal & Petroleum Products	1100	100	1200	1100	150	1250	1.0	1.5	0.6
Chemicals & Allied Industries	10	—	10	20	—	20	—	0.1	0.2
Metal Manufacturing & Metal Products	250	50	300	300	50	350	0.3	1.5	2.0
Industrial Plant & Steelwork	1250	150	1400	1900	250	2150	1.8	3.3	4.6
Miscellaneous Engineering	400	10	400	3850	400	4250	3.6	1.1	0.7
Ship Building, Boat Building & Marine Engineering	500	150	650	600	250	850	0.7	6.3	7.5
Vehicles	350	20	400	500	50	500	0.4	1.9	0.8
Textiles	10	—	10	50	10	50	—	1.7	3.3
Clothing, Footwear & Leather	850	650	1450	550	500	1000	0.8	2.8	2.2
Bricks, Pottery, Glass, Cement	50	300	350	40	300	350	0.3	1.7	1.9
Timber	450	100	550	500	200	700	0.6	0.8	1.2
Furniture, Office Fittings, etc.	500	30	550	500	30	550	0.5	0.5	0.4
Paper & Board Manufacturing	100	50	150	150	20	150	0.1	0.5	0.8
Paper & Board Products	750	100	850	800	100	900	0.8	0.5	0.3
Printing & Publishing	10	—	10	—	—	—	—	0.5	0.6
Other Manufacturing Industries	300	100	450	350	200	550	0.5	1.1	1.5
TOTAL MANUFACTURING	30	50	100	40	50	100	0.1	0.8	1.5
CONSTRUCTION	8552	2692	11244	12616	3483	16099	13.5	29.7	32.3
GAS, ELECTRICITY & WATER	10526	451	10977	16810	738	17548	14.7	7.9	5.6
Road Passenger Transport	1241	170	1411	1244	186	1430	1.2	1.4	1.5

Sea, Port & Inland Water Transport	1150	50	1200	900	50	1000	0.8	0.8	0.9
Air Transport	1300	100	1400	1300	100	1400	1.2	0.8	0.7
Postal Services & Telecommunications	150	10	150	400	50	450	0.4	0.2	0.4
Miscellaneous Transport & Storage	2350	1150	3500	2200	550	2750	2.3	1.7	1.9
Wholesale Distribution	50	20	50	150	100	250	0.2	0.7	0.7
Retail Distribution	850	250	1100	1200	400	1600	1.3	1.9	2.4
Dealing	3000	5700	8700	2800	7000	9800	8.2	8.6	8.4
Insurance, Banking & Business Services	550	100	700	900	200	1100	0.9	1.0	1.3
Educational Services	1400	850	2250	1700	1400	3100	2.6	3.8	5.1
Medical & Dental Services	1700	4750	6450	2600	6150	8750	7.3	7.9	8.2
Research & Development Services	1500	4650	6150	1700	5750	7450	6.2	6.9	5.7
Other Professional & Scientific Services	2000	300	2350	2150	350	2450	2.1	0.4	0.5
Sport & Other Recreation	400	650	1050	650	750	1450	1.2	1.7	1.6
Hotels, Other Residential Establishments	250	100	350	450	250	700	0.6	0.5	0.5
& Public Houses	2400	5500	7900	3400	6700	10100	8.5	3.4	2.3
Restaurants, Cafes, Snack-Bars	200	1000	1200	300	1200	1550	1.3	0.8	0.7
Catering Contractors	—	—	—	350	300	650	0.5	0.3	0.3
Garages & Filling Stations	1800	350	2150	2000	550	2550	2.1	1.9	2.0
Miscellaneous Services	800	2400	3200	1350	5750	7100	5.9	4.4	4.5
Public Administration & Defence	5500	1900	7400	6200	2900	9100	7.6	7.0	7.1
TOTAL SERVICES	29149	30140	59289	34094	39606	73700	61.7	56.9	57.3
GRAND TOTAL	60070	34392	84462	74571	44885	119456	100	100	100

Employment wholly related to North Sea Oil (largely included above)	H & I June 1977	Dec 1980
Primary (exploration/development/production)		490
Manufacturing (platform construction, engineering etc)		6,255
Construction		8,620
Services (transport, supplies, catering etc)		2,275
TOTAL	10,455	17,640

1—Industry totals for the Highlands and Islands are rounded to the nearest 50 employees, except those employing less than 50, which are rounded to the nearest 10.
2—Exclusion of the self employed is particularly significant in agriculture. If working occupiers, working wives and crofters putting in at least 40 man days per year are included the figure for 1977 for the Highlands and Islands rises to over 16,000.
3—Fishing employment is drawn from DAFS Creek Returns for the Highlands and Islands but from Department of Employment ER11 records for Scotland and Britain.
4—The figures exclude Arran and the Cumbraes.

Sources: Department of Employment
DAFS

Area unemployment profiles

Diagram 1 Appendix 4

Employment exchange areas 1980

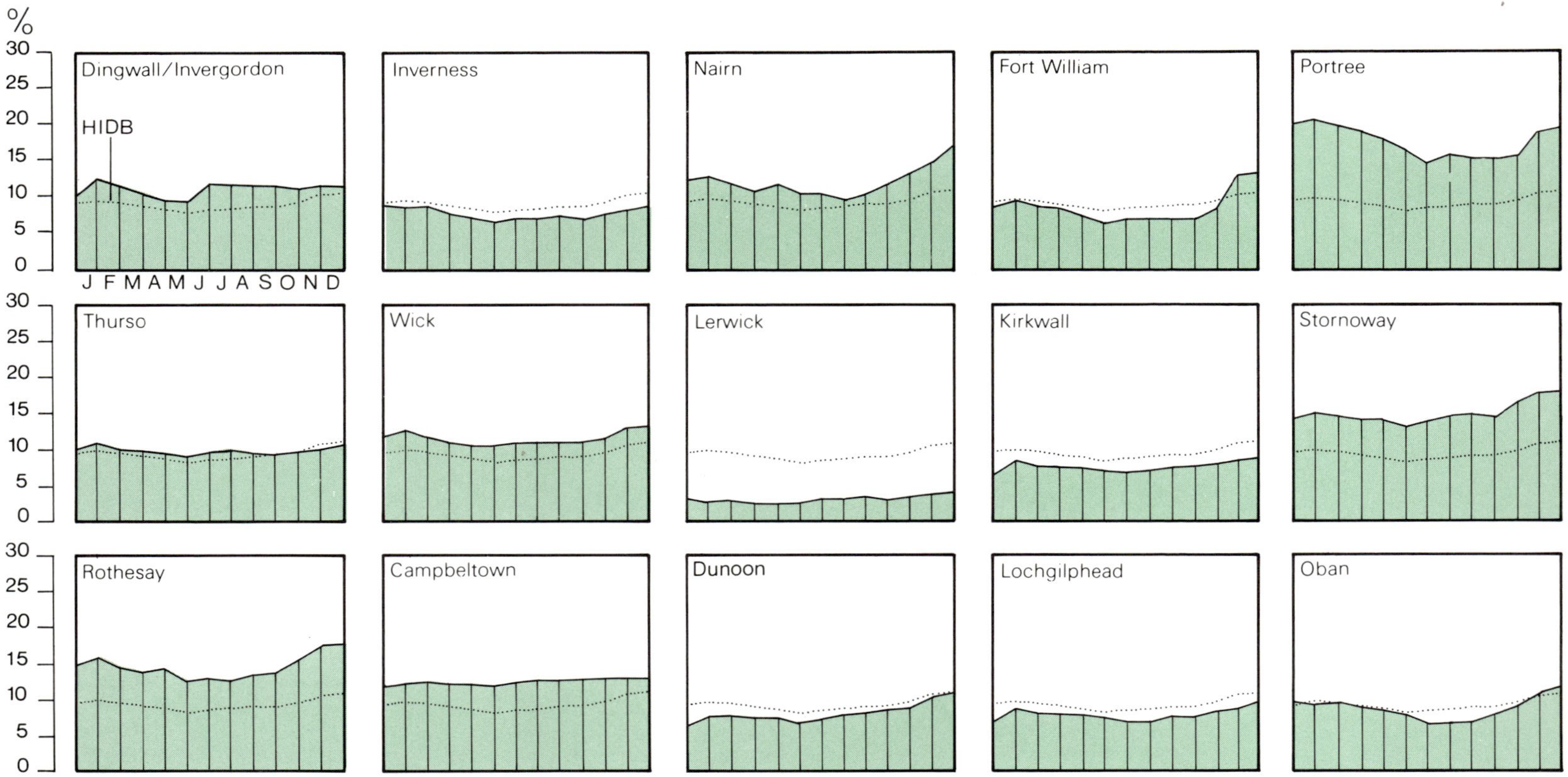

%
30
25
20
15
10
5
0

Dingwall/Invergordon
HIDB
J F M A M J J A S O N D

Inverness

Nairn

Fort William

Portree

Thurso

Wick

Lerwick

Kirkwall

Stornoway

Rothesay

Campbeltown

Dunoon

Lochgilphead

Oban

Source: Manpower Services Commission monthly unemployment data, unadjusted

Agriculture

Table 5 Appendix 4

	HIDB area				Scotland			HIDB as % of Scotland	
HECTARES (000's) under	1961	1971	1979	1980*	1961	1979	1980	1961	1980
Agricultural land	3,373.2	3,045.2	3,077.1	3,096.2	6,776.2	6,134.0	6,169.4	50	50
Rough grazings	3,131.0	2,825.9	2,815.9	2,832.1	5,032.3	4,366.6	4,384.3	62	65
Grass	168.9	165.8	177.1	179.0	1,122.6	1,060.6	1,066.8	15	17
Oats	42.1	21.0	8.8	9.4	255.9	36.5	38.2	16	25
Barley	6.0	18.0	36.1	35.6	129.8	436.4	443.5	5	8
Wheat	1.0	2.0	0.5	0.6	37.1	23.5	25.6	3	2
Potatoes	4.4	2.5	2.1	2.1	54.9	34.1	35.3	8	6
Vegetables for human consumption	0.07	0.07	0.11	0.12	4.8	8.2	8.7	1	1
Soft fruit	0.04	0.15	0.12	0.11	3.8	3.8	3.9	4.0	3
NUMBER OF LIVESTOCK (000's)									
Breeding ewes	1,274	1,109	1,016	1,047	3,604	3,051	3,159	35	33
Total cattle	313	343	390	383	2,045	2,398	2,383	15	16
Beef breeding herd	96	125	138	135	313	542	524	31	26
Dairy breeding herd	34	25	32	30	460	368	354	7	8
Poultry	1,113	438	324	241	9,181	12,743	13,303	12	2
Pigs	21	23	12	14	430	505	468	5	3

*1980 data include 1979 information for Arran and the Cumbraes

Notes:
Data are not strictly comparable because of statistical modifications by DAFS in 1970 and 1973.
From 1979 onwards, data refer to the north-west sub-region plus Argyll and Bute District and the islands of Arran and the Cumbraes (as defined by DAFS).

Source: DAFS (June census returns)

Fisheries

Table 6 Appendix 4

Catches by area and type of fish

FISHERY DISTRICTS	PELAGIC[1]		DEMERSAL[2]		SHELLFISH		TOTAL	
Weights of catches in thousands of tonnes	1979	1980	1979	1980	1979	1980	1979	1980
Lossiemouth (Nairn to Ardgay)	0.5	3.5	—	—	—	0.5	0.6	4.0
Wick	—	—	3.5	4.6	0.7	1.3	4.2	5.9
Lerwick	1.4	4.7	26.1	37.0	2.1	1.9	29.6	43.6
Stornoway	8.7	13.1	1.4	3.6	1.6	1.5	11.8	18.2
Ullapool/Mallaig	95.1	80.9	12.1	13.4	6.0	4.3	113.2	98.6
Oban/Campbeltown	1.4	2.5	3.8	3.5	5.3	6.2	10.5	12.2
HIDB area total	107.1	104.7	46.9	62.3	15.6	15.8	169.9	182.8
Scotland	124.8	120.5	201.9	223.2	28.2	27.6	354.9	371.3
HIDB area/Scotland %	85.8	86.9	23.2	27.9	55.7	57.2	47.9	49.2
Value of HIDB area catch £'000[3]	10,417	8,431	11,943	13,344	15,855	12,579	38,227	34,355

Notes:

1 Includes herring, mackerel, sprats and blue whiting
2 Includes cod, haddock, whiting etc
3 The values of the 1979 catches have not been adjusted for inflation between 1979 and 1980, which averaged 18%

Source: DAFS.

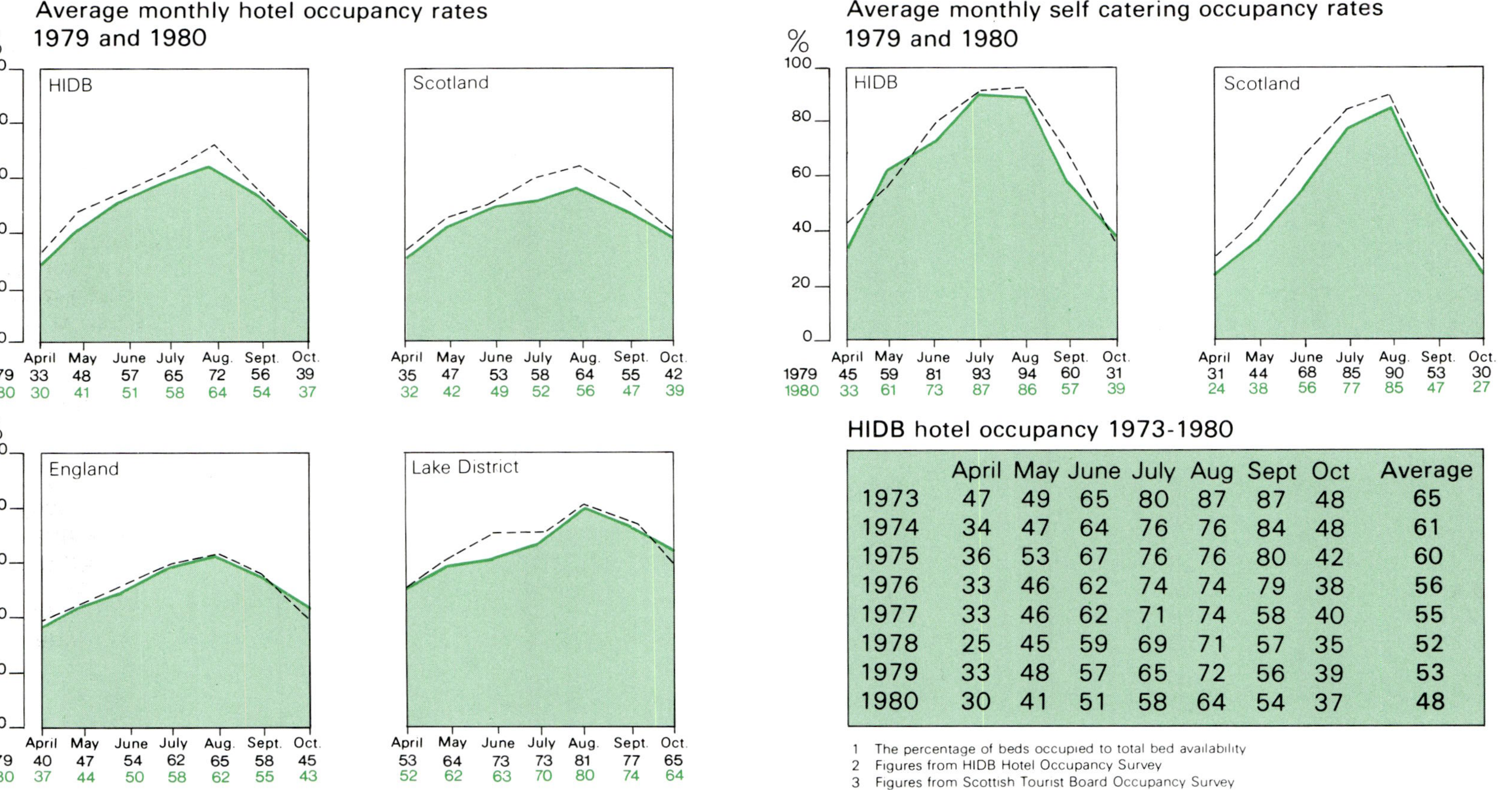

HIDB hotel occupancy 1973-1980

	April	May	June	July	Aug	Sept	Oct	Average
1973	47	49	65	80	87	87	48	65
1974	34	47	64	76	76	84	48	61
1975	36	53	67	76	76	80	42	60
1976	33	46	62	74	74	79	38	56
1977	33	46	62	71	74	58	40	55
1978	25	45	59	69	71	57	35	52
1979	33	48	57	65	72	56	39	53
1980	30	41	51	58	64	54	37	48

1 The percentage of beds occupied to total bed availability
2 Figures from HIDB Hotel Occupancy Survey
3 Figures from Scottish Tourist Board Occupancy Survey
4 Figures supplied by the English Tourist Board
5 The percentage of units occupied to total units available
6 Figures from HIDB Self Catering Survey and Scottish Tourist Board Survey of Self Catering Accommodation

Board assistance by statistical area 1980

Table 1 Appendix 5

Area	No. of cases	Approved Grants £	Approved Loans & shares £	Approved Social Development Grants £	Expenditure on board Projects £
Shetland	41	235,844	364,789	27,195	116,000
Orkney	112	358,048	529,911	33,455	183,000
Caithness	66	610,151	360,176	33,773	80,000
N.W. Sutherland	24	92,723	159,154	13,861	16,000
S.E. Sutherland	27	72,915	199,026	20,778	106,000
W. Ross	35	153,795	126,235	9,489	30,000
E. Ross	47	384,981	388,951	18,919	58,000
Inverness	63	588,644	399,642	16,492	1,060,000
Nairn	16	126,410	138,350	3,419	76,000
Badenoch	34	648,440	131,000	19,834	136,000
Lochalsh	11	56,401	64,435	1,000	1,000
Skye	43	137,788	225,604	9,138	536,000
Lewis & Harris	43	129,640	230,478	25,533	374,000
Uists & Barra	45	321,539	504,562	6,650	125,000
Lochaber	47	355,395	307,950	6,840	455,000
Argyll Islands	55	338,379	211,812	10,381	94,000
Oban & Lorn	47	569,275	346,481	15,620	17,000
Mid-Argyll & Kintyre	43	515,315	917,523	5,488	586,000
Dunoon & Cowal	25	226,903	150,650	6,435	240,000
Bute	19	237,909	212,000	1,656	235,000
Arran & Cumbraes	33	86,454	63,285	14,748	29,000
Non/area specific	6	—	—	10,044	631,000
TOTALS	882	£6,246,949	£6,032,014	£310,748	£5,184,000

NOTE: Board project expenditure does not include research, surveys and publicity.

Board assistance by statistical area 1971-80 (at 1980 prices)

Table 2 Appendix 5

STATISTICAL AREAS	No of cases	Grants £'000	Loans and shares £'000	Total £'000	Grant equivalence £'000	Employment created	Employment retained	Population (1974)	Grant Equivalence per head of population
Shetland	271	1,791	5,079	6,870	2,807	650	405	18,445	152
Orkney	480	2,498	5,472	7,970	3,592	727	298	17,462	206
Caithness	431	2,956	7,578	10,534	4,472	1,292	396	27,901	160
N.W. Sutherland	144	1,130	832	1,962	1,296	227	60	3,547	365
S.E. Sutherland	199	1,217	1,613	2,830	1,540	486	197	9,923	155
West Ross	236	2,623	2,489	5,112	3,121	524	110	4,632	674
East Ross	248	2,331	4,280	6,611	3,187	1,486	125	33,534	95
Inverness	299	5,594	6,194	11,788	6,833	2,145	386	51,897	132
Nairn*	40	428	426	854	513	91	15	8,906	58
Badenoch	166	2,983	1,438	4,421	3,271	612	144	9,043	362
Lochalsh	40	300	249	549	350	77	14	2,379	147
Skye	244	2,068	2,480	4,548	2,564	501	109	7,340	349
Lewis & Harris	297	2,881	6,960	9,841	4,273	1,291	697	23,073	185
Uists & Barra	193	1,973	3,192	5,165	2,611	463	187	6,987	374
Lochaber	320	4,669	4,511	9,180	5,571	1,262	287	19,150	291
Argyll Islands	290	2,865	2,958	5,823	3,457	506	192	7,368	469
Oban & Lorn	236	2,850	2,142	4,992	3,278	631	191	13,619	241
Mid Argyll & Kintyre	313	4,465	7,615	12,080	5,988	1,379	360	18,612	322
Dunoon & Cowal	149	1,985	2,076	4,061	2,400	619	216	17,315	139
Bute*	64	615	842	1,457	783	250	37	7,956	98
Arran and Cumbraes*	109	507	515	1,022	610	150	27	4,787	127
Non-area specific	12	27	326	353	92	9	0	—	—
TOTAL	4,781	48,756	69,267	118,023	62,609	15,378	4,453	313,876	199

NOTES:
The figures above relate to assistance approved by the board — not payments. Cases withdrawn after approval are thus included.
Social development grants are excluded.
Grant equivalence is defined as grant + one fifth loan.
Part-time or seasonal jobs are valued at half a job and part-time seasonal jobs at a quarter.

*Nairn, Bute and Arran were not eligible for board assistance until 1975 and the Cumbraes until 1980.

Board assistance by sector 1971-80

Table 3 Appendix 5

(at 1980 prices)

	Grants (£)	Loans & Shares (£)	Employment created	Employment retained
Land development	3,439,600	11,339,298	894	584
of which: Farm development	1,372,680	8,289,979	361	390
Horticulture	362,323	689,537	143	35
Fisheries	5,808,041	22,012,159	1,350	440
of which: Fishing boats	2,314,767	19,574,014	1,018	342
Fish farming	3,223,952	1,944,790	273	83
Manufacturing & processing	10,035,389	18,221,673	6,502	1,845
of which: Fish processing	1,278,693	2,925,784	962	398
Boatyards & marine engineering	620,527	1,306,494	295	195
Crafts	941,187	1,350,690	1,175	180
Construction	1,429,683	3,255,098	1,317	490
Tourism	24,464,905	10,453,891	3,719	754
of which: Hotels	11,714,738	5,332,242	1,842	509
Other tourist accommodation	7,341,439	2,591,463	702	93
Catering	1,467,002	782,620	602	16
Recreation and tourist amenities	3,544,868	1,683,297	537	132
Other service industries (exludes tourism and services directly related to land development and fisheries)	3,578,394	3,984,908	1,596	339
Total	£48,756,012	£69,267,027	15,378	4,452

Notes:
The figures above relate to assistance approved by the board — not payments. Cases withdrawn after approval are thus included.
Part-time or seasonal jobs are valued at half a job and part-time seasonal jobs at a quarter.

Total jobs created and retained

Table 4 Appendix 5

by board assisted developments since 1971

Years	Total jobs created	Total jobs retained
1971-75	6,993	1,143
1972-76	7,411	1,537
1973-77	7,664	1,889
1974-78	8,028	2,417
1975-79	8,186	3,355
1976-80	8,533	3,309

NOTE: Part-time or seasonal jobs are valued at half a job and part-time seasonal jobs at a quarter.

Commissioned enquiries, investigations and researches

Appendix 6

Completed or underway during the year ended 31 December 1980
(Section 9 (1)(c) of the Act)

SURVEY	BY	
Area Development		
Survey of the impact of industrial growth in Easter Ross: environmental and land use survey	*Department of Geography, University of Aberdeen*	In progress
Research on migration and development in the Highlands and Islands	*Institute for the Study of Sparsely Populated Areas, University of Aberdeen*	Completed
Price survey in remote areas	*Institute for the Study of Sparsely Populated Areas, University of Aberdeen (commissioned in conjunction with Scottish Consumer Council)*	In progress
Study into the opportunities to create new jobs in the Fort William area	*Job Creation Ltd*	In progress
Fort William industrial study	*Coopers and Lybrand Associates Ltd*	In progress
Investigation of the indirect economic impact of the closure of the chemical pulp mill at Corpach	*Scottish Council Research Institute*	Completed
Research on social indicators within the Highlands and Islands	*Department of Geography, University of Dundee*	In progress
Implications of micro-electronic technology for industry in the Highlands and Islands	*PA Management Consultants Ltd*	Completed
Transport		
Transport and distribution of goods in the Highlands and Islands	*Department of Town and Regional Planning, University of Glasgow*	In progress
Market research study of potential for freightliner/speed link rail services in the Highland Region, Orkney and Shetland	*M & M Distribution Consultants (commissioned in conjunction with Highland Regional Council and British Rail/Freightliner Ltd)*	Completed
Industrial Development and Marketing		
Analysis of the cost of factory building in the Highlands and Islands	*Glasgow College of Building and Printing*	In progress
Study of the demand by employers for training facilities in Mid Argyll and Kintyre	*Scottish Council Research Institute Ltd (commissioned in conjunction with Manpower Services Commission)*	Completed
Identification of American electronics companies with potential for development in the Highlands and Islands	*El Tronics International Incorporated*	In progress
Assessment of new range of products for geological and similar applications	*Dr Masson Smith of Institute of Geological Sciences*	Completed

Assessment of market potential of metal detectors in four European countries	*Industrial Market Research Ltd*	In progress
Assessment of market for PAN oxidised fibre	*Hipertech — Mr D R Lovell*	Completed
Natural gas liquids from the North Sea gas gathering system	*Chem Systems International*	Completed

Tourism

Accommodation booking analysis	*University Computing Company (Great Britain) Ltd*	Completed
Assessment of the feasibility of establishing a purpose-built angling centre in the Highlands and Islands	*Research Bureau Ltd*	Completed
Study of the potential for water sports development in Argyll and Bute	*LSD Leisure and Recreation Ltd (commissioned in conjunction with Argyll & Bute District Council)*	Completed
Study of the potential for water sports development in Arran and Cumbrae	*LSD Leisure and Recreation Ltd*	In progress
Survey of visitor expenditure in the Highlands and Islands during 1980	*Research Bureau Ltd*	In progress
Survey on the cost of converting property in Rothesay to self/catering accommodation	*National Building Agency (in conjunction with Scottish Tourist Board and Argyll & Bute District Council*	In progress

Fisheries

Investigation and development of underground water resources for fish hatcheries and farms	*Highland Fish Farmers Ltd*	In progress
Feasibility study on the use of thermal infra-red data in locating shoals of fish	*University of Dundee*	In progress
Investigation of the fishery pecten maximus in Loch Creran	*Heriot Watt University (PhD studentship)*	In progress
Two-year programme to evaluate the potential for oyster cultivation, Isle of Colonsay	*A M Abrahams*	Completed
Shellfish research programme	*Scottish Sea Farms Ltd*	In progress
Extension of research programme to evaluate the potential for scallop cultivation	*J J Walford*	In progress
Evaluation of Loch Teacuis, Rahoy for fish farming	*Argoventure Ltd*	In progress
Study on the problems of bacterial kidney disease in salmonids	*University of Aberdeen (PhD studentship)*	In progress
Research into the castration of rainbow trout and salmon	*University of Stirling*	Completed
Evaluation of the Maricult Flotation 'stud-on' system of oyster attachment	*Scottish Sea Farms Ltd*	In progress
Mussel cultivation in Caol Scotnish and Loch Sween	*Scottish Marine Biological Association in conjunction with J & A Kay (Caol-Scotnish) Ltd*	Completed
Crab processing in the Uists	*M Branagan and H Stewart in association with Torry Research Institute (MAFF)*	In progress
Investigation into feasibility of establishing small-scale trout units in Lewis and Harris	*C C E Bayly*	In progress

Research programme into site suitability for shellfish cultivation and evaluation of sites in the board's area	*G C MacKay BSc*	In progress
Ardveenish Harbour	*Babtie Shaw and Morton*	In progress

Land

Study on fuel peat production in Caithness	*I Miller and N Godsman*	Completed
Venison production in the Highlands and Islands	*A B Cooper*	In progress
Grazing trial for North Ronaldsay sheep	*North of Scotland College of Agriculture*	Completed
Direct drilling trials of turnips and swedes — Tiree	*West of Scotland Agricultural College*	Completed
Feasibility of growing soft fruit in the West of Scotland	*Applecross Organic Fruit Farm*	In progress
Investigation into the suitability of baled and bagged silage for Uist conditions	*Crofters from North and South Uist and Benbecula in conjunction with North of Scotland College of Agriculture*	In progress
Mechanised peat cutting	*Lews Castle Technical College*	In progress
Establishment of potato breeding programme	*Dr J M Dunnet*	In progress
Sheep improvement programme, North Ronaldsay	*North of Scotland College of Agriculture*	In progress
Survey of muirburn practice in relation to sheep and game performance in west Scotland	*Dr A N Lance NCC (commissioned in conjunction withthe Nature Conservancy Council and Game Conservancy)*	In progress
Marketing of venison in West Germany	*University of Stirling (MSc studentship)*	Completed
Study of nutrition and lactation in red deer hinds	*University of Edinburgh*	Completed
Study of carcase composition of farmed red deer	*Rowett Research Institute*	Completed

In addition to the studies commissioned directly, the board participated in the following studies commissioned or carried out by other bodies:

SURVEY	COMMISSIONED BY	
Marine fish farming research programme at Ardtoe	*White Fish Authority*	In progress
Investigation of phytoplankton and fish kills in Loch Striven	*Scottish Marine Biological Association in conjunction with University of Stirling*	In progress
Draft fishing plan of the Orkney Islands area	*Orkney Islands Council & Orkney Fisheries Association*	Completed
Evaluation of fish cages constructed of copper nickel mesh	*International Copper Research Association Ltd in conjunction with Highland Fish Farmers Ltd and Wester Ross Salmon Ltd*	In progress
Research programme to evaluate the potential for shellfish cultivation in the Orkney Islands	*Orkney Islands Council*	In progress
Investigation of the impact of the Greenland fisheries on the United Kingdom salmon resource	*Atlantic Salmon Research Trust and the International Atlantic Salmon Foundation*	Completed

Feasibility study to examine the prospects for co-operation in production and marketing	*Highland Horticultural Group (carried out by T Fleming Associates)*	In progress
Study into feasibility of establishing a local abattoir and meat industry in Kirkwall	*Orkney Islands Council and FMC (Scotland) Ltd*	Completed
Site investigation at Corpach Moss, Fort William	*Scottish Development Agency and Highland Regional Council (carried out by Jamieson MacKay and Partners)*	Completed
Rural public transport studies	*East Ross and Black Isle Council of Social Service and North and West Sutherland Council of Social Service (carried out by Department of Geography, University of Aberdeen)*	In progress
Study in conservation and development — Highland fisheries	*Highland Regional Council*	Completed
Research into oyster cultivation methods in Loch Sween	*University of Glasgow (PhD studentship) under the Science Research Council's Co-operative Awards in Science and Engineering (CASE) Scheme*	In progress
Regional impact of biomass energy sources in Scotland	*DGX11 of Commission of the European Communities partly sponsored by Scottish Development Agency and HIDB (carried out by General Technology Systems Ltd)*	In progress
Research project to identify sites for public viewing of rare birds	*Royal Society for the Protection of Birds*	In progress
Eden Court Theatre financing	*Eden Court Theatre (carried out by Coopers and Lybrand Associates Ltd)*	Completed

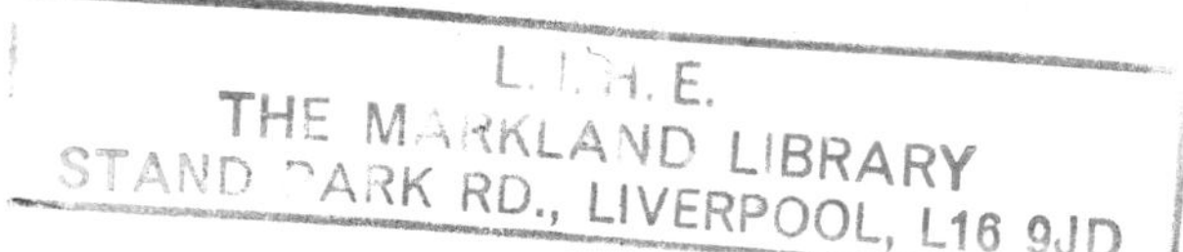

Membership of Highlands and Islands Development Consultative Council

Appendix 7

for the period 1 January 1980
to 31 December 1980

Chairman
Professor Sir Robert Grieve, FRSE

Members
C W Blumfield, OBE
* G D Brims
A R Budge
Mrs A Burnett
Lt Col A E Cameron, MC
A J Cluness
F M Cook, OBE
* P Drummond
R W Edwards
E R Eunson
* Col A M Gilmour, OBE, MC
A Halliday
* D R Hayes
B T Hunter
W Leonard (from 1.8.80)
A A McCreevy (from 1.8.80)
R MacFarquhar
F Macintosh
D Mackay
D J Mackay
J K MacKay
A C McLean
* Lt Col H McLean, MBE
T MacKenzie, OBE, MM (to 31.3.80)
N I MacLean
C Macleod, OBE
Mrs F MacLeod (from 1.8.80)
D L MacMillan
D J McPherson
Mrs M H MacPherson
H Matheson
Mrs E Munro
Mrs M C Murchison
A J Murray
C Neilson (to 31.7.80)
H A Patience
W P Reid
A B Robertson (from 1.8.80)
I G Russell (from 1.4.80)
B M Scott
* Mrs E M Sillars, MBE
C Spencer
G Stevenson (from 1.8.80)
J C Stuart (to 31.7.80)
* Col J Taylor, MC, TD
E Thomason (from 1.8.80)
C T Wardman (to 31.7.80)
Rev J Callan Wilson (to 31.7.80)
J Wilson (from 1.8.80)
E Young

Secretary
T H John

* Reappointed for a further term.

Acknowledgments

Produced and published by the Highlands and Islands Development Board, Inverness, May 1981.

Printed by Nevisprint Ltd, Fort William.

Designed by Jim Thomson Graphic Design, Muir of Ord.

Cartography by Wendy Price, North Kessock.

Photographers — Tom Cameron, Clyde Surveys Scotland Ltd, Anthony MacMillan, Oscar Marzaroli, Northern Studios, David Sim, Angus Smith, Eric Thorburn, George Young.

This book is to be returned on or before
the last date stamped below.

Local Authority Areas